STUDY GUIDE SI

THE NEW TESTAMENT

GALATIANS TO PHILEMON

Freshly translated by Nicholas King

kevin mayhew

For William and Abigail,
with love

First published in 2006 by
KEVIN MAYHEW LTD
Buxhall, Stowmarket, Suffolk, IP14 3BW
E-mail: info@kevinmayhewltd.com
www.kevinmayhew.com

The text for *Galatians to Philemon* first appeared in Nicholas King's translation of *The New Testament*.

9 8 7 6 5 4 3 2 1 0

ISBN 1 84417 547 2
Catalogue No. 1500898

Cover Design: Jonathan Stroulger
Editors: Peter Dainty, Marian Reid
Typesetting: Richard Weaver

Set in Simoncini Garamond and *Abadi MT Lt It*

Nihil Obstat: This translation has been examined by the Theology Committee of the Bishops' Conference of England and Wales and is declared free from doctrinal error. It is not authorised for use in the Liturgy of the Church and is approved for publication, in accord with Canon 825§1.

Mgr Andrew Summersgill, General Secretary, 8 June 2004

Printed and bound in Great Britain

Contents

Introduction

The order in which the letters attributed to Paul appear in our New Testaments has nothing to do with the order in which they were written; it is simply that 'longest comes first'. So in this second volume of translation and commentary we shall be reading the shorter ones, from Galatians, which is full five chapters, down to the charming post-card that is the Letter to Philemon. What holds them all together is the sudden and disconcerting discovery Paul had made, that it was all true about Jesus, that Jesus was risen, that Jesus had now to be worshipped as 'Lord', and that he, Paul, now had a mission from Jesus to the non-Jews. This was a remarkable turn-around for one who had hitherto made it his mission to put an end to the claims of those who asserted that Jesus was alive. He went into it, however, with characteristic gusto, and with all the restless creativity of his intellect. One of the privileges that we have as we read Paul's letters is to watch his mind at work as he wrestles with the implications of this earth-shattering discovery and tries to talk business with the at times rather awkward members of the churches that he had founded.

It is true that some of the letters in the Pauline corpus are judged by many scholars not to be from Paul's hand. These would include, in varying degrees of uncertainty, 2 Thessalonians, Ephesians, Colossians, 1 and 2 Timothy and Titus (although it has to be said that some scholars would make a case for all of these letters to have been written by Paul). Even if Paul did not write them, they are clearly evidence for the kind of thing that his immediate successors felt he would be saying 'if he were alive today'. And simply wrestling with the text and asking 'could Paul have written this?' is a useful discipline which can teach us much about this prickly and passionate theological genius who was head over heels in love with Jesus.

It may be helpful to keep in mind the structure of letters in the ancient world. We tend to begin a letter with the name of the addressee ('Dear X'), and only put our name at the end ('Yours Ever, Fred', or whatever). In the ancient world (perhaps more logically) the author's name comes first, followed by greetings to the addressees, then a thanksgiving to the gods, followed by the main business of the letter, and finally the closing greetings. Paul always follows this pattern, except that in Galatians he is so cross that there is no thanksgiving. The difference is that Paul really makes the main body of the letter work for him; that is where he puts all the difficult theological argumentation. So Paul's letters are not exactly like other letters in the ancient world, but a creative improvement on the established practice, to cope with the new reality that came into his life when he met Jesus.

Galatians is clearly a very ill-tempered letter: his Christians have got things so badly wrong, and are trying to undo Paul's 'gospel of freedom'. Some scholars think that it was Paul's first letter; certainly it seems to be among his earliest.

Ephesians is for many people the loveliest letter in the Pauline corpus. It clearly has some relationship to Colossians, but more scholars attribute Colossians to Paul than think that Paul wrote Ephesians. All agree, however, that the author of Ephesians understood Paul very well, so perhaps it doesn't matter all that much! And there are scholars who are quite prepared to assign Ephesians to Paul. The blessing that comes after the opening greeting is, you may be interested to learn, the longest sentence in the entire New Testament.

Philippians, though written from prison, at a time when Paul didn't know whether he would get out alive, is by some way the most cheerful of his letters: 'rejoice in the Lord at all times; and again I shall say: rejoice' is almost thematic in this letter. I sometimes think that the Christians at Philippi may have been Paul's favourite community. Notice, though, that even at Philippi there was quarrelling among those earliest Christians, or at least between Evodia and Syntyche (4:2).

Colossians, like Ephesians, which in several respects it resembles, is sometimes thought to be written by a follower of Paul in the next generation. It is a lovely letter, though it is hard at this distance to be sure what false beliefs the author is attacking. Colossians is also linked in some way with Philemon, the last and smallest letter in the Pauline canon.

1 Thessalonians may well be Paul's earliest letter, which gives it therefore some claim on our attention as representing perhaps the first words of the New Testament. As you read it, ask why it is that people write letters, and why Paul wrote this one. Part of the answer is that it is often the next best thing to being present in person; but for Paul it is also a way of helping to solve the problems that have arisen in churches that he had founded, during the time he had been away from them. Notice that there are problems in Thessalonica concerning those who had died. It looks as though Paul may have preached to them a doctrine of a fairly imminent Second Coming of Jesus; but if some of their number had died, did that mean that they had missed out on being with Christ? Watch how Paul answers the implied question.

2 Thessalonians is sometimes regarded as being by someone other than Paul – the argument is that it stays too close to 1 Thessalonians, using it merely as a platform for attacking the view that 'Jesus has already come'. The question it deals with is a tricky one: how do we spend our time, as we wait for Jesus' return? The answer is: 'get on with your work'.

Next come the three 'Pastoral Letters', 1 and 2 Timothy and Titus. Very few scholars (though there are some) think that Paul wrote these letters. They are unusual, in that they are addressed to individuals rather than churches (not even Philemon is addressed to just a single person); and they show a concern for church order and orthodoxy that many people regard as unlikely for the lifetime of Paul. The vocabulary seems different, too; but it is important to read these letters with an open mind, and there is much profit to be had from them.

Last but not least there is the Letter to Philemon, a delightful and tiny piece, which I sometimes think is the place to start with when getting to know Paul.

For that is your task as you read this book: get to know Paul, that great lover, whose love for Jesus turned the world upside down and forced him to invent a new way of writing and talking. Whether or not these letters were all written by Paul, all of them have much to tell you about that prickly and difficult character, about the vicissitudes of the earliest attempts at living Christianity, and above all about the one without whose Risen Presence none of these letters would have been written: the one whom Paul knew as 'Lord'.

The Letter to the Galatians

The Letter to the Galatians

This is, it has to be said, a very ill-tempered letter. Some scholars regard it as Paul's first surviving work (though a majority would give the accolade to 1 Thessalonians). In this letter, Paul covers the same issues (what God has done in Christ) as in Romans, but with considerably less diplomatic skill. One of the great joys of this letter is that Paul is forced to tell us a good deal about his faith-journey.

Opening greeting

1 1-5 Paul, an apostle (not [appointed] by human beings, or through any human being, but through Jesus Christ, and through God the Father, who raised him from the dead), and all the Christians who are with me, to the churches of Galatia, grace to you and peace from God our Father and the Lord Jesus Christ, who gave himself for our sins, that he might rescue us from the present evil age, according to the will of our God and Father, to whom be glory for ever and ever. Amen.

For Paul, the opening greeting is never a mere formality; words are always made to work. Notice his insistence that he is an apostle, whose appointment has no human source, but is authenticated by God and Jesus Christ; note, too, Paul's insistence on the link between his mission and the Resurrection. Paul does not here mention anyone else as joint author of the letter, but characteristically stresses that it comes from 'all the Christians who are with me'; the letter, dealing with mighty matters, is not just his own. Nor is it addressed to particular awkward individuals, but to 'the churches of Galatia'. As always, Paul wishes his readers 'grace' and 'peace', words which carry a great weight of meaning; they are not just idle religious platitudes. In connection with this, we should note that Paul believed that you could detect a clearly visible transformation when people became Christian. So when he speaks of 'rescue' from 'the present evil age' he has solid content in mind. Notice, finally, how God the Father has been mentioned several times in this short greeting.

What might Paul mean by 'rescue us from this present evil age'?

What, no thanksgiving?

6-9 I am astonished that you are so quick to turn away from the one who called you in Christ's grace, to another gospel. ***There is no other gospel***:* but there are people who are unsettling you, and who are aiming to pervert Christ's gospel. No – even if we ourselves, or an angel from heaven were to preach you a gospel different from the gospel that we preached to you, let them be accursed! We have said it before, and now we are saying it again: if anyone preaches the gospel to you contrary to the gospel that you received, ***let him or her be accursed***.

* Words in bold throughout the text are my emphasis

In all Paul's other letters, the opening greeting is followed by a thanksgiving, which acts as a kind of foretaste of the themes of the letter. In Galatians, however, he is so cross with what has been going on in Galatia that he substitutes 'I am astonished' for the expected 'I thank God'.

What is it that has gone wrong? They have abandoned 'the gospel (he) preached', the gospel of 'grace', for a different gospel. Paul expresses his fury at this by solemnly cursing anyone who preaches the 'perverted' gospel, even if it should be himself or 'a messenger of God', as he suggests, with more than a touch of exaggeration.

We can be grateful, however, to those who got the gospel wrong, because they forced him to remind the Galatians of elements of his faith-journey, which we should otherwise not have known. He tells the story in three sections.

What is 'the gospel' that Paul defends so passionately? Would we today be sure to recognise when it was not being preached?

Paul's faith-journey: first section

10-17 Am I now trying to win over human beings or God? Or am I seeking to please human beings? If it were still human beings that I were trying to please, I should not be a slave of Jesus Christ. I want you to know, brothers and sisters, the gospel that was preached by me: it was not of human origin. I didn't receive it from human beings, nor was I taught it by them. No – it came through a revelation of Jesus Christ.

You've heard of my manner of life once upon a time within Judaism, how violently I used to persecute God's Church, and how I tried to destroy it, and how I made progress within Judaism beyond many of my contemporaries who were of the family; I was far more fanatical about the ancestral tradition. But when it was God's good pleasure (God who had marked me out from my mother's womb and had called me through his grace) to reveal his Son to me, that I might preach the gospel [about] him to the Gentiles, I didn't immediately consult with human beings; and I didn't go up to Jerusalem to [see] those who were apostles before me. Instead, I went off to Arabia, and came back again to Damascus.

We may guess from this that someone had been accusing Paul of concentrating too much on human beings, and not enough on God. Certainly he is emphatic that what happened to him came from God. Hence the word 'receive', which Paul uses elsewhere to describe the tradition that he wishes to defend, and the emphasis that it 'came through a revelation of Jesus Christ'. As in the opening of Romans, he calls himself a 'slave of Jesus Christ', as a title that he and the Galatians can agree about. For Paul, the reality that matters is Jesus, and nothing else; and for Paul 'Jesus' includes, in one direction, God (source of his vocation) and, in the other direction, the Church, which Paul had been persecuting. This must guide our interpretation of the two references to Judaism in this passage. It was not that Paul thought of himself as an 'ex-Jew' or a convert from Judaism; Romans 9-11 makes it clear that he still thought of himself as very much a Jew. What had made all the difference was a personal encounter with Jesus Christ, and his consequent belief that God had raised Jesus from the dead, and then his sense of being called to preach God-in-Jesus to all the world, beyond the bounds of Judaism. Note that Paul regards himself as an apostle on just the same level as the Twelve ('those who were apostles before me').

Why is Paul so keen to emphasise that his gospel has 'no human source'?

Paul's faith-journey: second section

18-24 Thereafter, after three years, I went up to Jerusalem, to visit Kephas; and I remained a fortnight with him. I saw none of the other apostles, except for James the brother of the Lord.

(Look – what I am writing to you, before God, I am not telling lies.)

After that I came back to the regions of Syria and Cilicia. The churches of Judaea that are in Christ did not know me by sight; they had only heard that 'our one-time persecutor is now preaching the gospel of the faith, which once he tried to destroy' – and they glorified God in me.

The autobiography continues. The point here is how little contact he had with the Twelve, just a fortnight with Peter after three years in Arabia or Damascus, and a session (perhaps no more) with James the brother of the Lord. Where had Paul learnt the gospel? Basically, he is claiming, from the risen Jesus.

Why did the churches of Judaea 'glorify God' in Paul?

Paul's faith-journey: third section

2 1-10 Then, fourteen years later, I went back to Jerusalem, taking Barnabas and Titus with me. I went up in accordance with a revelation. And I put before them the gospel which I proclaim among the Gentiles (but privately, to the 'influential ones': I didn't want my present and past efforts to be useless). But they didn't even make my companion Titus (he was a Greek) get circumcised. However, because of some fake Christians who had been smuggled in – they had sneaked in to spy on our freedom that we have in Christ Jesus. Their aim was to reduce us to slavery; but we didn't give in to them even for a moment. We wanted the gospel's truth to remain continually with you.

Now from the so-called 'influential ones' (it makes no difference to me what kind of people they once were; God is not a snob) . . . for the 'influential ones' made no addition. No, on the contrary, seeing that I was entrusted with the gospel of uncircumcision, just as Peter was [entrusted with the gospel] of circumcision (for the One who had worked in Peter, for his mission to the circumcised, had worked also in me for the Gentiles); and when they realised that [God's] grace had been bestowed on me, James and Kephas and John, the so-called 'pillars', gave me and Barnabas the right hand of fellowship: we were to go to the Gentiles, and they to the circumcised. The only thing was, we were to remember the poor – and I was eager to do that very thing.

Some of the sentences in this passage are incomplete, or lose their way, which may be an indicator of how passionately Paul feels the issue as he dictates.

This third stage covers a huge period of time; very likely the visit to Jerusalem that he mentions here is the same as that referred to in Acts 15, but scholars are divided about it, and it need not worry us. What Paul is emphasising is, first, his independence from the 'influential ones' and his dependence on God. Second, Paul insists on his vocation to preach to non-Jews, just as Peter (does he only call him Kephas when he wants to keep him in his place?) had the vocation to preach to Jews. The instruction at the end to 'remember the poor' is something that Paul refers to also in Romans, as well as in the two Corinthian letters that we have. It was very important to him.

What does Paul mean here by 'slavery'?

Confronting Kephas's hypocrisy: first statement of the gospel

11-21 But when Kephas came to Antioch, I opposed him in person, because he stood condemned. For before the arrival of some people from James, he used to eat with Gentiles. But after their arrival, he drew back and held himself aloof – he was terrified of the circumcision people! And all the rest of the Jews joined him in playing the hypocrite, so that even Barnabas was led to join in their hypocrisy. But when I saw that they were not advancing in the direction of the truth of the gospel, I said to Kephas, in front of all of them, 'If you, who are Jewish by race, no longer live according to Jewish custom, how come you are forcing Gentiles to become Jews? You and I are Jews by nature, not sinners of Gentile stock. We know that a person is not made righteous by works of the law, but by faith in Jesus Christ. And we have come to faith in Jesus Christ, that we might be made righteous by Christ's faith, and not by works of law: because no human being is made righteous by works of law. Now – if we, who seek to be made righteous in Christ, ourselves turn out to be sinners, does that mean that Christ is a servant of sin? No way. For if I start building up all these things that I pulled down, then I show that I am a transgressor. For through law I died to law, in order that I might live to God; I have been crucified along with Christ. But now I live [and it is] no longer I, but Christ lives in me. The life I now live in the flesh, I live in faith in the Son of God, who loved me, and who gave himself up for my sake. I do not make God's grace null and void; for if righteousness comes through law, then Christ's death is in vain.'

It is reassuring, somehow, to find these distinguished apostles locked in controversy. The Greek does not tell us where Paul's speech to Peter ends, and where the theological comment begins. My translation opts to take the theological argument as part of what Paul said to Kephas, inviting the Galatians to listen in on the argument, and so to grasp it for themselves, before he turns on them.

The word 'hypocrite' originally means an actor, someone who plays a part that is not really his or hers.

Why does Paul oppose Peter?

You stupid Galatians!

3 1-5 You ***stupid*** Galatians – who has bewitched you? It was before your eyes that Jesus Christ was exhibited as crucified. Tell me just this one thing: the Spirit – did you get it from works of law or from obedience to the faith? Are you so stupid? You made your beginning in the Spirit – are you now coming to an end in the flesh? Have you experienced so much for nothing? (That's assuming that it ***was*** for nothing.) Look – the one who laid the Spirit on for you and worked miracles among you, was that the result of works of law or of faith in what you heard?

Paul is very cross: most Christian pastors avoid addressing their flock in language quite as strong as this, but Paul thinks that the Galatians are in life-threatening danger of missing the point. And notice that it is Paul's assumption that he could appeal to their experience of having 'seen' Christ crucified, and of having the 'Spirit'. For Paul, the Christian experience is tangible, palpable; Paul takes it for granted that they had actually seen things happening when he first was among them.

'It was before your eyes that Jesus Christ was exhibited as crucified.' What does this mean?

The argument from Abraham

6-29 Just as Abraham 'believed God, and it was reckoned to him as righteousness' [Genesis 15:6], you know that those who are 'of faith' are the ones who are children of Abraham. However, Scripture foresaw that God [would] reckon the Gentiles as righteous as a result of faith, and gave Abraham a foretaste of the gospel: 'in you all the Gentiles will be blessed' [Genesis 12:3]. So that those who are 'of faith' are blessed along with faithful Abraham.

You see, all those who are of law-works are under a curse. For it is written 'accursed is everyone who does not abide by all the things that are written in the book of the law, so as to perform them' [Deuteronomy 27:26]. Now it is clear that no one can be made righteous before God by the law, because 'the righteous one by faith shall live' [Habakkuk 2:4]. Now the law is not 'by faith'; but 'those who do them shall live by them' [Leviticus 18:5]. Christ has bought us back from the law's curse; he became a curse for our sake, because it is written, 'cursed is the one who is hanged on a tree' [Deuteronomy 21:23], in order that Abraham's blessing might extend to the Gentiles in Christ Jesus, in order that we might receive the promised Spirit through faith.

Brothers and sisters, I am speaking in a human way. Likewise [or: 'nevertheless'] no one sets aside a will that has been ratified, or adds a codicil to it. Now the promises were uttered 'to Abraham and to his seed' [Genesis 12:7]. It doesn't say 'to his seed***s***', in the plural; no, it's in the singular, 'and to your seed', and that is Christ! This is my argument: the will [or: covenant or: Testament] that had already been validated by God ***can't*** be set aside by the law (which came 430 years later), so as to annul God's promise. You see, if the inheritance is a matter of law, it's no longer a matter of promise: it is to Abraham that God has shown himself gracious through the promise.

So what is the law? It was an added extra, because of transgressions, until the 'seed' should come to whom the promise had been made; it was ordered through angels, by the agency of a mediator. Now you can't have a mediator where there is only one party – and God is one.

'So the law is in contradiction to the promises of God?' No way! Because if the law that was given had the power to bring life, then indeed righteousness would be 'from the law'. Instead, law locked up everything under sin, so that the promise which is the fruit of Jesus Christ's faith is given to those who have faith.

However, before faith came, we were held in custody under law, locked up [to wait] for the faith that was destined to be revealed. So the law became our instructor, leading us to Christ, so that we might be made righteous by faith. But when faith came, we are no longer under the instructor. For you are all children of God, through the faith that was in Christ Jesus; you see, as many of you as were baptised into Christ, you have put on Christ. There is no such thing as Jew or Greek, no such thing as slave or free, no such thing as male and female. For you are all one in Christ; and if you belong to Christ, then you are the 'seed of Abraham', heirs according to [God's] promise.

The argument is difficult, but perhaps would have been more easily grasped by the Galatians, who had heard Paul talk, than by us. We have always to remember that Paul did not expect us to be reading this letter, so he has not given us the key to crack its code.

Clearly, though, the person of Abraham is important. He was an iconic figure, as the ancestor of all Jews, but he was not yet circumcised when he was 'justified by faith' (so faith is prior to circumcision or works of law); and second, Abraham's blessing was for 'all Gentiles' (or nations). Third, and the argument is stretched thin here, 'seed' is in the singular, not the plural, and therefore (according to Paul) was referring to one of Abraham's descendants in particular, namely Christ.

Paul has to hold together two not wholly compatible positions, that law is the gift of God, and that law is limited; so he hints at the idea that law (or Torah) is a 'teacher' (with all the negative emotions that idea can arouse). Much more important, though, is that the law is not Christ, around whom everything revolves for Paul; and if baptism (see how Paul keeps coming back to the Galatians' own experience) is a matter of 'putting on Christ', like an actor's costume, then all human divisions, ethnic (Jew or Greek), cultural (slave or free) and sexual (male and female) are irrelevant. What counts is, quite simply, the promise of God.

Notice that three of the Old Testament citations (those from Genesis 15:6, Habakkuk 2:4, and Leviticus 18:5) are used again at important moments in the argument of Romans (4:3, 22, 23; 1:17; 10:5). Romans is Paul's second, and more diplomatic, attempt at defending the case he makes in Galatians. It is interesting to note that Paul clearly expected his Galatian converts (Gentiles as well as Jews) to know the Jewish scriptures, and to accept arguments based on them.

Is there a difference between hypocrites (remembering that the word means 'actors') and Christians, who 'put on Christ', like actors?

Argument from the law, about an heir who is still a minor

4 1-11 This is my meaning: while the heir is a minor, he is no better than a slave, even though he is master of everything; he is under guardians and house managers until the time set by his father. So with us: when we were 'minors', we were enslaved under the elemental spirits of the universe. When, however, the fullness of time came, God sent out his Son, born of a woman, born under law, in order to buy back those under law, that we might receive adoption-as-sons. But because you are sons, God sent the Spirit of his Son into our hearts, crying 'Abba, Father'. So you are no longer a slave; you are a ***son***. Now, if you are a son, then you are an heir, through [what] God [has] done.

But at that time, you did not know God, and you were enslaved to what were not really gods at all. Now, however, you know God – or rather you are known by God – how is it that you are reverting to the weak and destitute elemental spirits? Why do you want to be enslaved to them all over again? You are religiously observing days and months and special feasts and holy years. I fear for you – perhaps my labour for you was in vain!

The analogy of a son (and I fear that there is no way here of maintaining inclusive language and still preserving the force of Paul's argument; but it is only an analogy) who has not yet entered into his inheritance is presumably meant to illustrate what was wrong with the law: it was not the real thing, but only a teacher. The real thing is what God (Father) has done for us, by sending the Son and Spirit, who enable us to cry 'Abba, Father'. The Galatians are being asked to remember what it was like before they met Christ, and not to revert to their old captivity.

Paul is anxious that the Galatians are 'religiously observing days and months and special feasts and holy years'. Might he level a similar charge against us?

Reviewing the relationship between Paul and the Galatians

12-20 Be like me, my fellow Christians, I implore you, because I was like you. You did me no wrong; but you are well aware that it was because of a weakness of the flesh that I preached the gospel to you the first time; and you didn't despise the [trial that I experienced] in my flesh. Nor did you vomit [spit] me out: no – you received me as God's messenger, as Christ Jesus! So where is your happiness now? For I swear to you that, if possible, you would have dug out your eyes and given them to me. So have I become your enemy, by telling you the truth?

Their cultivation of you is not honourable; they want to lock you up, so that you can cultivate them! But it is honourable to be cultivated in an honourable way all the time, and not just when I'm with you. My children: I am suffering birth-pangs with you until Christ is formed among you. But I wanted to be present with you now, and adapt my tone to you – I'm puzzled about you.

Paul is annoyed with his Galatians; but also there is no mistaking the affection he has for them; and he can appeal to the happy memories that they share: 'if possible, you would have dug out your eyes and given them to me,' he says of their first meeting. Some readers have deduced from this that Paul was suffering from a disease of the eyes; they point to the 'big letters' of his handwriting (see 6:11), and suggest that an eye disease may have been the 'thorn in the flesh' of 2 Corinthians 12:7, and even link it to Paul's allegedly unimpressive presence, referred to in 1 Corinthians 2:3 and 2 Corinthians 10:10.

The reference to 'spitting out' might suggest either disdain or a gesture to ward off evil spirits.

'I'm puzzled about you.' Why is Paul 'puzzled'?

Slave and free: Hagar and the mother of Isaac

21-31 Tell me, you who are so keen on being under the law – don't you listen to the law? For it is written that Abraham had two sons, one from the slave girl and one from the free woman. But the one born of the slave girl was born according to the flesh, while the one born of the free woman [was born] through the promise. This is an allegory – for the women are the two covenants, one from Mount Sinai, born into slavery, and that's Hagar. Now Hagar is Sinai – a mountain in Arabia; it corresponds to present-day Jerusalem, because, along with its children, it is in slavery. Whereas the Jerusalem [which is] above is free – that is our mother. For it is written,

'Rejoice, O barren woman, who does not give birth.
Break out and shout, you who have no birth-pangs.
For many are the children of the deserted one,
more than the one who has a husband' [Isaiah 54:1].

Now you, brothers and sisters, are children of the promise after the manner of Isaac. But just as the one born according to the flesh used to persecute the one born according to the Spirit, so it is now. But what does Scripture say? 'Expel the slave girl and her son; for no way will the son of the slave girl inherit on equal terms with the son of the free woman' [Genesis 21:10-12]. So, brothers and sisters, we are not children of a slave girl, but of the free woman.

It is striking that in this comparison, deeply offensive to many Jews, Paul does not mention the name of Sarah, but only that of Hagar. The point that he is trying to make is that the Galatians are actually looking to go back into the slavery from which the gospel of Jesus has rescued them. It is an ingenious and bold stroke of Paul to use Abraham's wife and concubine to illustrate his argument.

Why does Paul speak of 'slavery' here?

Freedom and circumcision

5 1-12 By [this] freedom, Christ set us free; so hold your ground, and don't go back to being burdened by the yoke of slavery.

Look, I, Paul, am telling you that if you are circumcised, Christ is of no use to you. My testimony for every man who is circumcised is that he is under an obligation to perform the whole law. You have been estranged from Christ, you who find your righteousness in the law; you have fallen away from [God's] gift. For ***we***, by the Spirit and as a result of faith, are waiting eagerly for the righteousness that we hope for. For in Christ Jesus, neither circumcision nor uncircumcision is of any use – no, [what matters is] faith, achieving its effects through love.

You were running nicely: who impeded you, so as not to obey the truth? That persuasion does not come from the One who called you. A little leaven leavens all the dough. I am confident in you in the Lord, that you will not think any differently: whoever he is, the one who is unsettling you will carry the blame. As for me, brothers and sisters, if I proclaim that circumcision still matters, why am I being persecuted? So the scandal of the Cross is eradicated.

I wish that those who are disturbing you would castrate themselves.

The last line (which will have offended many to whom it was reported) shows how passionately Paul views the issue. For him what was wrong with the law was that it was not Christ, and therefore insisting on obeying the law's precepts simply meant undoing all that Christ had done for them.

Paul has clearly been accused of still giving importance to circumcision (hard though that may be to credit); but his 'bottom line' is the 'scandal of the Cross'.

What does Paul mean by the 'scandal of the Cross'?

Spirit and flesh

13-26 For, my brothers and sisters, you were called to be free; but don't let your freedom become an opportunity for your unreformed humanity. Instead, be each other's slaves through love. For the whole law is fulfilled in a single saying, in 'You shall love your neighbour as yourself' [Leviticus 19:18]. But if you are biting and devouring each other, watch out that you aren't consumed by each other.

I'm telling you: walk in the Spirit, and absolutely do not yield to the desire of the flesh. For the desire of the flesh is against the Spirit; that of the Spirit against that of the flesh: for they are opposed to each other. I don't want you to be doing the things that you don't want to be doing.

If you are led by the Spirit, you are not under the law. The works of the flesh are evident: sexual immorality, impurity, debauchery, idolatry, drugs, outbursts of hatred, quarrelling, fanaticism, fits of rage, outbreaks of selfishness and dissension, factions and envy, drunkenness and revelry, and all that sort of thing.

I am giving you advance warning, as I have already done, that people who do that sort of thing will not inherit God's kingdom.

The fruit of the Spirit, on the other hand, is love, joy, peace, patience, kindness, goodness, faith, gentleness and self-control. There is no law against that sort of thing. Those who belong to Christ Jesus have crucified the flesh along with [its] passions and desires. If we live by the Spirit, let us also follow the Spirit. Let us not turn into empty-heads, provoking each other and envying each other.

It is important here to keep our eye on what really matters for Paul: belonging to Christ Jesus, being willingly crucified with him, accepting the Spirit. And, of course, we have to make a choice: are we to go with the flesh or with the Spirit? That was what the Galatians were failing to do when they flirted with law observance, as far as Paul is concerned.

Paul gives a list of 'works of the flesh' and 'fruit of the Spirit'. If you were making the list, what examples would you add to either column?

Why are 'works' and 'fruit' appropriate metaphors for these two categories?

General instructions

6 1-10 Brothers and sisters, if a person is caught out in some transgression, you are of the Spirit, so set him right in a spirit of gentleness; and keep an eye on yourself, in case you get tempted. Carry one another's burdens, and in this way you will fulfil the law of Christ. For if a person thinks they are something, when they are nothing, they are fooling themselves. Let everyone test their own work, and then they will have reason for boasting over themselves, not over the other person. For everyone will carry his or her own load.

Let the teacher of the word teach his or her pupil in everything that is good. Don't be misled – God is not to be outwitted. You see, what a person sows is what they will reap; because the person who sows in the field of flesh will bring in a harvest of destruction from that source, while the person who sows in the Spirit's field will bring in a harvest of eternal life. Let us not grow weary of doing what is good, for when our own time comes we shall bring in a harvest, provided that we don't slacken. So then, since we have our opportunity, let us do good to all, but especially to those in the family of the faith.

We only hear one side of the 'telephone conversation' between Paul and his Galatians, and we need to remember that fact whenever we are inclined to dismiss these closing instructions as weary religious clichés ('hate evil and do good'). Paul does not waste words, and we have to assume that these instructions will have had a very precise meaning to those who were more aware of the problems that the Galatian churches were experiencing.

'Keep an eye on yourself, in case you get tempted.' What is Paul saying here?

In his own write

11-18 Look what big letters I'm drawing for you in my handwriting! All those who want to make a good showing in external matters are the ones who are trying to force you to get circumcised, just so as to avoid being persecuted for the cross of Christ. You see, not even the circumcised keep the law – but still they want you circumcised, so that they can boast of your flesh! As for me, may I never boast on any grounds but those of the Cross of Our Lord Jesus Christ, through whom the world is crucified to me and I to the world. For circumcision is irrelevant, and uncircumcision is irrelevant: what matters is 'new creation'; and all those who follow this rule, peace upon them, and mercy, and on the Israel of God.

For the rest, let no one cause me problems. For I carry the scars of Jesus on my body.

The grace of Our Lord Jesus Christ be with the spirit of you all, my brothers and sisters. Amen.

The phrase 'new creation' is an important idea for Paul. He uses the phrase, for example, at 2 Corinthians 5:17. The idea of the 'new human' appears in Ephesians 2:15; 4:24 and Colossians 3:10 (but not everyone agrees that both of these letters are by Paul). The idea is also lurking, probably, beneath the text of Romans 6:4; 7:6; 8:2, 21. 'In Christ', there is no longer the polarisation of the world in which Paul had grown up, between 'Jews' and 'non-Jews'. What matters now is simply a new symbolic universe, without the old identity markers, which the Galatians and Paul have experienced and can refer to as a 'new creation'. Galatians and Romans cannot really be understood apart from this idea.

It looks as though Paul wrote all these last verses out with his (rather unskilled) hand. As he brings this angry letter to a close, notice his emphasis on the Cross of Christ, and his sense of sharing in Christ's sufferings, all in order to encourage the Galatians not to abandon the gospel that he had preached. Notice also Paul's sense of mission ('the world is crucified to me, and I to the world'); and ponder his remarkable phrase 'the Israel of God'.

Galatians was written for a particular crisis in a particular Church. What does it have to say to us today?

The Letter to the Ephesians

The Letter to the Ephesians

This is a very different letter from its predecessors, and there is uncertainty about whether it was written by Paul, and whether it was in fact written to Ephesus; this need not worry us too much. Certainly, though, its style is fuller than what we are accustomed to in Paul. There are elaborate groups of nouns strung together, and the sentences are rather long. I have tried, not entirely successfully, to make these long sentences more manageable by the use of bullet points. Someone who was quite at home in Paul's thought wrote this document. It is a letter of great richness, and steeped in the liturgy of the early Church. It is many people's favourite Pauline epistle.

Opening greeting

1 1,2 Paul, an apostle of Christ Jesus, through the will of God to the saints who are
[at Ephesus], and to those who are faithful in Christ Jesus, grace to you and
peace from God our Father and the Lord Jesus Christ.

As is frequently the custom today, I have left the addressee town in brackets, as a reminder of the uncertainties in the manuscripts and among the early witnesses. Otherwise this is a standard opening to a Pauline epistle.

Blessing

3-14 Blessed be the God and Father of our Lord Jesus Christ,

- the one who blessed us with every spiritual blessing in the heavenly regions in Christ, just as he chose us in him before the foundation of the world, for us to be holy and unblemished before him in love,
- the one who predestined us for adoption-as-sons through Jesus Christ to him, according to the good pleasure of his will, to the praise of the glory of his grace with which he graced us in the Beloved,
- the one in whom we have redemption through his blood, the forgiveness of transgressions according to the wealth of his grace, which overflowed to us, in all wisdom and understanding,
- the one who revealed to us the mystery of his will, according to his good pleasure which he proposed in him, for the plan for the fullness of times, recapitulating everything in Christ, the things in the heavens and the things on earth,
- in him in whom we have our lot cast, in accordance with the design of the one who carries out everything, according to the plan of his will, so that we should be for the praise of his glory, we who have been the first to hope in Christ,
- in whom you also have heard the word of truth, the gospel of your salvation,
- in whom you believe, and have been sealed with the Holy Spirit of promise, which is the down payment of our inheritance, for the redemption of the [God's] property, to the praise of his glory.

This section is an immense single sentence and the longest in the entire New Testament (but by no means the last long sentence we shall encounter in Ephesians); and you have to admire the way in which the author has held it together, with a series of no less than seven relative clauses, four referring to God the Father, and three referring to Christ, which we have signalled with a series of bullet points, to show how it all works. It is a lovely hymn of praise, and even when we cannot follow in detail what the author is saying, we can nevertheless sit back and relish his profoundly spiritual theology. You will notice the series of nouns, often turned into adjectives by translators, which marks the style of the author of this epistle, such as, for example, 'to the praise of the glory of his grace'. This piling up of nouns gives density to the language and depth to the spiritual theology of the epistle.

This 'blessing' comes where we should normally expect to find the thanksgiving in a Pauline letter. That thanksgiving perhaps now follows.

The fourth 'bullet point' speaks of the 'mystery of his will' and of 'recapitulating everything in Christ'. Many people have been inspired by the mystical vision of God gathering everything into Christ. Does it help you to open up to God's work in our world? (You might like to look at Paul's remarks about the 'groaning' of creation in Romans 8:19-23.)

Thanksgiving (or is it?)

15-23 Because of this, I too, having heard of the faith that is among you in the Lord Jesus, and the love for all the saints, do not cease from giving thanks, making remembrance of you in my prayers,

- that the God of our Lord Jesus Christ, the Father of glory, may give you a spirit of wisdom and revelation in the knowledge of him, the eyes of your heart enlightened so that you may know
- what is the hope of his calling,
- what is the wealth of the glory of his inheritance among the saints,
- and what is the overarching greatness of his power for us who believe according to the exercise of the might of his strength,
- which he exercised in Christ [by] raising him from the dead, and making him sit on his right hand in the heavenly regions, above all rule and authority and power and lordship, and every name that is named, not only in this age, but also in the coming age,
- and 'he subordinated everything beneath his feet', and gave him as head over the entire Church, which is his body, the fullness of that which fills everything in every respect.

This is another immense sentence, and we may feel, as we admire the rich theology of it, that the author has overdosed on nouns once more. It is easier to stand back and admire the broad picture he paints than to stand close and work out the detail; and it must be admitted here that our attempt to pick out the structure of the sentence by the use of bullet points is less successful than in its predecessor. The word translated as 'Church' is a very important one in Ephesians, and there is something to be said for taking it, slightly more literally, as 'Assembly', except that it does not work quite so well in every instance in this letter; but whenever you see it, the reader should bear in mind the slightly different nuance that the word 'assembly' offers.

The citation in the final bullet point, 'he subordinated everything beneath his feet', comes from Psalm 8:6, where it refers to the authority of human beings over all creation (see Genesis 1:26, 28). Interestingly, both here and at Hebrews 2:8, 9, it is made to refer to Christ. Jesus of course often referred to himself as Son of Man, which might account for this rather free use of the psalm.

What does it mean to call Christ 'head over the Church which is his body'?

What God has done for the readers

2 1-10 And you, who were dead because of your transgressions and sins,

- in which once you walked in keeping with the age of this world, in keeping with the ruler of the power of the air, the spirit that is now at work among the children of disobedience
- among whom we all once lived because of the desires of our flesh, doing the wills of the flesh and of the intellects, and we were by nature children of anger, just like the rest,
- but since God is rich in mercy, because of the great love with which he loved us,
- and us who were dead because of transgressions

he made alive together with Christ

(It is by God's gift that you have been saved)

and raised you with him

and made you sit in the heavenly regions in Christ Jesus

in order that in the coming ages he might demonstrate the surpassing value of his free gift in kindness to you in Christ Jesus.

For it is by [God's] free gift that you have been saved through faith – and it has nothing to do with you; it is God's gift. It is not dependent on what you have done (so that no one should boast). For we are his 'poem', created in Christ Jesus for good works, which God prepared in advance, so that we might walk in them.

The reader is here invited to be astonished at the generosity of God, to feel its impact on his or her life, and to concentrate on the central building-blocks of Pauline belief, that a) God raised Jesus from the dead, b) the Resurrection has a clearly visible impact on the lives of Christians, and c) that this is not because Christians have been particularly deserving, but because of God's loving generosity. I have put the key phrases in bold italics, to simplify the reader's task.

The reader may like to know that the word 'poem' is simply a transcription of what Paul wrote. It might equally be translated as 'work of art'.

What does the author of Ephesians think that God has done for us in Christ?

Remember what you once were, and where you are now

11-22 Therefore recall that once you were Gentiles, in unredeemed human nature, those who are called 'uncircumcision' by the so-called 'circumcision' (which is in the flesh, made by human hands),

- that you were at that time separated from Christ, alienated from the commonwealth of Israel, strangers to the covenants of the promise, hopeless and godless in the world,
- but now in Christ Jesus you who were once far off have come near in the blood of Christ.

For he is our peace, who in his flesh made the two into one, and has dissolved the dividing wall that acts as a fence, the hatred,

- who has cancelled out the law of commandments that consisted of regulations
- so that he might thereby fashion the two into a single human person, making peace and reconciling the two to God in a single body through the Cross, putting the hatred to death in [Christ].

And he came and preached the gospel of peace to you who were far off, and peace to those who were nearby, because through him both of us have, through a single Spirit, access to the Father.

So therefore you are no longer foreigners and strangers. No – you are fellow-citizens of the saints, and members of the family of God, built upon the foundation of the apostles and prophets, with Christ Jesus himself as the cornerstone,

- in whom the whole building is crafted together and grows into a holy temple in the Lord
- in whom you are built up into God's dwelling place in the Spirit.

The long sentences of Ephesians are not really what we are used to in the letters that are certainly written by Paul, and it is important to take them slowly, to make sure that you see how they work; use the bullet points to find your way into the structure. Notice, though, that the ideas owe a good deal to the thinking that Paul has already done: the uniting of Gentiles and Jews, the tension between the two, the tangible difference that Christ makes, the centrality of Jesus, his death-resurrection and his peace, the cancellation of the law, the metaphor of a building, the emphasis on the Spirit, and the extraordinarily rich and powerful idea of the Church as the Body of Christ. All these are ideas that are already in 1 Corinthians and Romans.

'So therefore you are no longer foreigners and strangers.' Into what have Christians been transferred, according to this doctrine?

The difference that the gospel makes, to those who preach and to those who hear

3 1-7 For his sake, I, Paul, a prisoner of Christ Jesus, on behalf of you Gentiles (assuming that you have heard of the stewardship of God's grace that was given me for you),

- because by a revelation the mystery was made known to me, as I have written briefly above, in accordance with which you are able to read and comprehend my understanding in the mystery of Christ
- which in earlier generations was not made known to the 'sons of men'
- as now it is revealed to his holy apostles and prophets by the Spirit,
- for the Gentiles to have a share in the inheritance, and in the body, and in the partnership of the promise in Christ Jesus through the gospel
- of which I became a minister, according to the free gift of the grace of God, which was given to me according to the activity of his power.

This is not difficult to understand, but quite hard to translate. At times one feels that the author has only a tenuous grasp on his clauses, which seem about to fly off in all directions. The sentence starts 'I, Paul', but we are never introduced to the main verb that this leads us to expect.

Many readers will anxiously ask if there is not some dishonesty in the author pretending to be Paul, if indeed this document is not written by the apostle. It may be helpful to think of a successor of Paul, one who knows his thought well, telling the reader or hearer, 'this is what Paul would be telling us today', rather than to worry about a forger trying to deceive us.

Is it something for us to worry about, if it turns out that Paul did not in fact write this letter?

The apostle's ministry summed up

8-13 To me, the least significant of all the saints, this grace was given, to preach to the Gentiles the unfathomable wealth of Christ, and to shed light

- on what is the stewardship of the mystery which had been hidden from the ages by the God who fashioned everything
- that the many-sided wisdom of God might be made known now to the powers and authorities in the heavenly regions, through the Church according to the purpose of the ages which he fashioned in Christ Jesus our Lord,
- in whom we have full assurance and free access in confidence through his faith.

Therefore, I beg you not to despair at my afflictions on your behalf, which is your glory.

This is the verdict on Paul's apostolic task, and we can hardly follow (but must try to follow) the author as he scales mystical heights, the obsession with God, and the astonishment at what God has done, and his sense of where the Church fits into the picture.

What is the job of the apostle, according to Ephesians?

The apostle's prayer

14-21 For his sake I bend my knees to the Father,

- from whom all fathering in heaven and on earth is named,
- that he might grant you, in accordance with the wealth of his glory, to be mightily strengthened through his Spirit with regard to the 'inner person',
- that Christ should dwell through faith in your hearts,
- [that you may be] rooted and founded in love that you may have the strength
- to comprehend with all the saints
- what is the breadth and length and height and depth, to know
- the overarching love of Christ which transcends knowledge,
- that you may be filled with regard to all the fullness of God.

To the one who is able above all, quite beyond all measure of what we ask or understand according to the power that is at work in us, to him be the glory in the Church and in Christ Jesus to all generations for ever and ever. Amen.

This beautiful prayer clearly comes from the same hand as has constructed the rest of the letter, with its complex sentences and piles of nouns; but more important than that for the reader is the certainty about the accessibility (to all!) of the mystery of God in Christ. As with Paul's undisputed letters, God and Christ and love are right in the centre of the author's intention.

'The overarching love of Christ which transcends knowledge'. What does the author mean by this? What might it mean for us today?

Unity in the Spirit of the Body of Christ

4 1-16 Therefore I beg you, I who am the prisoner in the Lord, to walk worthily of the calling to which you have been called, with all humility and gentleness, with patience, putting up with one another in love, being eager to keep the unity of the Spirit, in the bond of peace: One body and one Spirit (just as you were called in one hope of your calling), one Lord, one faith, one baptism, one God and Father of all, who is over all and through all and in all.

To each one of us the grace is given according to the measure of Christ's free gift. Therefore it says,

> 'Going up to the height, he took captivity captive;
> he gave gifts to human beings.'

Now what is 'he went up', other than that 'he went down' to the lower regions of the earth? The one who 'went down' is the same as the one who 'went up', far above all the heavens, that he might fill everything.

And he himself gave some as apostles, others as prophets, others as evangelists, others as shepherds and teachers, for the equipping of the saints for a work of service, for the upbuilding of the Body of Christ, until all of us arrive

- at the unity of faith and the knowledge of the 'sons of God',
- at the perfect human being,
- at the measure of the stature of the fullness of Christ,
- so that we may no longer be infants, tossed here and there by waves, and carried here and there by every breeze of teaching, by the craftiness of human beings, by readiness to do anything bad as regards deceitful scheming,
- but that we may be truthful in love and make everything grow into him, who is the Head,
- Christ, from whom the whole body is joined together and knit together, through every supporting ligament according to the activity that is proper to each individual part;
- it may bring about the increase of the body for its own upbuilding in love.

Once again, it is reasonably clear what the author means here, though it is less obvious how the individual parts hang together. Three principles are affirmed here:

1. *the unity of the Church in the Spirit*
2. *the identity of Christ, now in glory, with the One who 'came down' to earth*
3. *the intimate connection of Christ and the Church (seen as Body of Christ).*

The quotation in the second paragraph, 'Going up to the height . . . ' is from Psalm 68:18, where it celebrates God's ascent to Mount Zion (or perhaps Mount Sinai); God's reign is symbolised by the fact that he **received** *slaves and other gifts. Here it is applied to Jesus, triumphantly entering heaven; and the wording has been changed, rather daringly, so that he now gives gifts.*

Who is Christ, for the author of this letter?

How to behave in the Body of Christ

4 17–5 20 This is my statement, and my testimony in the Lord: no longer [ought] you to walk as the Gentiles walk, in the futility of their intellects, being darkened in [their] understanding, alienated from God's life because of the ignorance that is in them because of the hardness of their hearts, who have become devoid of feeling and given themselves over to debauchery, to the practice of every kind of impurity to excess.

You, however, did not learn Christ that way (assuming, that is, that you ***did*** hear him and ***were*** taught in him) as the truth is in Jesus, for you to set aside the person you once were, according to your previous way of life, a person on the way to destruction according to deceptive desires. Instead, get yourselves renewed in the spirit of your mind and put on the new person, the one who is fashioned according to God, in the righteousness and holiness of truth.

Therefore put away falsehood, 'let each one speak truth with their neighbour' [Zechariah 8:16, freely cited], because we are parts of each other, 'be angry, but do not sin' [Psalm 4:5, freely cited]. Let the sun not go down on your anger, and do not give space to the devil. Let the thief stop stealing, rather let him labour, producing good with his own hands, that he may have something to share with the one who has need.

Let no evil speech come from your mouth; but nothing other than good [speech], to build [people] up in case of need, in order that it may give grace to those who hear.

And do not grieve the Holy Spirit of God, by whom you are sealed for the Day of Redemption. Let all bitterness and passion and anger and clamour and blasphemy be taken away from you, along with all that is evil. Be kind to one another, compassionate, forgiving each other, just as God in Christ forgave you.

So become imitators of God, like beloved children, and walk in love, just as Christ loved us and handed himself over for our sakes as an offering and a sacrifice to God, to make a fragrant smell.

Sexual immorality and all kind of impurity or excess should not even be named among you, as is fitting for holy people – and the same goes for wickedness and foolish talk or dirty jokes, which ought not to happen, but rather thanksgiving. For be quite certain that no one who is sexually immoral or impure or covetous (that's idolatry) has an inheritance in the kingdom of Christ and of God.

Let no one fool you with insubstantial talk; for this brings the wrath of God on the children of disobedience. Don't go into partnership with them: for once upon a time you were darkness. Now, however, you are light in the Lord – walk as children of the light, for light's fruit is all about goodness and righteousness and truth; test what is pleasing to the Lord, and don't go shares in the unfruitful works of darkness – instead [you should] expose them. For the things that are secretly done by them are too disgusting to mention, while everything that is exposed by the light is revealed, because everything that is revealed is light. Therefore it says,

'Awake, you who sleep
and arise from the dead,
and Christ shall shine upon you.'

So look carefully at how you are behaving: not as [the] unwise but as [the] wise, making the most of the time, because the days are evil. Therefore do not become foolish, but [try to] understand what is the Lord's will. And don't get drunk on wine, in which there is dissipation, but be filled with the Spirit, talking to yourselves in psalms and hymns and spirit-filled canticles, singing and playing musical instruments in your heart to the Lord, always giving thanks for everything in the name of our Lord Jesus to [our/his] God and Father.

This is a very long section on the kind of behaviour that is appropriate in the Body of Christ. Once again, the sentences are long, but never quite fly out of

control. The moral teaching is far more diffuse, far less precise, than in Paul, and yet the author shares the apostle's sense of what does and does not fit if you are Christians.

The lines 'Awake, you who sleep . . . ' may be a fragment of an early Christian hymn, or, just possibly, a loose translation of Isaiah 60:1, 'Arise, shine, for your light has come and the glory of the Lord has risen upon you.' Our author is quite free in his handling of the Old Testament.

Would you add anything to this list of behaviour that is acceptable and unacceptable for Christians?

How Christian families are to operate

5:21–6:9 Be submissive to one another in the fear of Christ:

- ***wives*** to their own husbands as to the Lord, because the husband is the head of the wife, as also Christ is the head of the Church – he is the Saviour of the body. But as the Church is submissive to Christ, so also wives to their husbands in every respect.
- ***husbands***, love your wives, just as Christ loved the Church, and gave himself for her, so that he might make her holy by the washing in water, accompanied by a form of words, that he himself might present the Church to himself as resplendent, with no stain or wrinkle or anything like that, but that she might be holy and blameless. That is how husbands ought to love their own wives, as their own bodies. The one who loves his own wife loves himself. For no one ever hates his own flesh, but nourishes and cherishes it, as Christ [does with] the Church, because we are limbs of his body. 'For this reason, a man will leave his father and his mother and will cling to his wife, and the two will become one flesh.'

This is an enormous mystery – and I am speaking of it with reference to Christ and to the Church. But you too, individually, let each of you love his own wife as you love yourself – but the wife should revere her husband.

- ***children*** – obey your parents in the Lord; for this is right: 'honour your father and your mother', which is the first commandment in the promise, 'that it may be well with you, and you may have a long life on the earth'.
- And ***parents*** – don't make your children angry, but look after them with the Lord's discipline and admonition.
- ***slaves*** – obey those who are your 'lords' according to the flesh, with fear and trembling, in simplicity of your hearts, as though [they were] Christ, not as doing your service to attract attention, as though you were 'pleasing people' – but as Christ's slaves, doing God's will from the heart, doing your slavery with enthusiasm, as for the Lord, and not for human beings, confident that whenever each one does anything good, they will get this from the Lord, whether they are slave or free.
- And '***lords***', do the same to them; give up menacing [them], confident that your Lord and their Lord is in heaven; and there is no snobbery in him.

The 'household code' is always a tricky passage to handle. It is our belief, of course, that all are equal before God, and many readers, properly anxious about the rights of women, children and slaves, are dismayed by what they read as a sanctification of a 'hierarchy of relationships' in the Body of Christ.

But look again. What the author of this epistle does in the 'household code' is to relativise all that his contemporary society would have taken for granted. It starts with a command of universal submission (not just women, slaves, children) 'in the fear of Christ', and all that follows serves only to relativise human hierarchies. So just as husbands, parents, and slave owners are turning to their 'inferiors' and saying 'Did you hear what the man said?', they find themselves under review: 'husbands, love your wives . . . as your own bodies'; 'parents – don't annoy your children'; 'slave-lords . . . know that their Lord and yours is in heaven'. We are not to read this simply as reinforcing the social stratification of contemporary society: the mention of 'love' rules that out.

Notice the instruction to children and parents; it looks at first like a simple quotation from Exodus 20:12 and Deuteronomy 5:16; but our author is quite daring in expecting it to include the responsibility of parents to their children, not to make them angry!

Does the use of the word 'love' in this passage make a difference to the teaching, in your opinion?

Concluding prayer: the 'suit of armour'

10-20 For the rest, be strong in the Lord, and in the might of his power. Put on God's suit of armour, so as to be able to stand against the devil's craftiness, because our struggle is not against blood and flesh; no – it is against the rulers, the powers, the world rulers of the present darkness, against the spirit forces of evil in the heavenly regions.

For that reason, take up God's suit of armour, that you may be able to resist on the Evil Day, and having won through against everything, to stand firm. So stand firm, with your loins girded with truth, and putting on the breastplate of righteousness, and putting sandals on your feet in readiness for the gospel of peace; in everything taking up the shield of faith, by which you will be able to extinguish all the Evil One's incendiary devices. And accept the helmet of salvation, and the sword of the Spirit, which is God's word.

Praying in all prayer and supplication, on every occasion in the Spirit, and for that reason staying awake in all patience and in supplication for all the saints – ***and*** for me, that I may be given speech when I open my mouth, to make known with complete confidence the mystery of the gospel, for which I am an ambassador-in-chains, so that in him I may utter freely, as I ought to speak.

Much of this is the slightly fanciful analogy of the 'suit of armour', which has so seized the Christian imagination. Notice the powerful sense that the author has, that Christians are engaged in a real battle, the importance of prayer, and (once again) the absolute centrality of God, and the mission to preach the gospel.

Do you feel embarrassed by all the military language that the author applies here to Christian life? Many people would say that this is because we have forgotten that Christian life is a battle against the evil powers. What 'evil powers' might there be ranged against Christians today?

Final salutations

21-23 But that you may know about me (what I'm up to), Tychicus, the beloved fellow-Christian, and faithful minister in the Lord, will tell you everything. I have sent him to you for this very purpose, that you may know about us, and that he may comfort your hearts.

Peace to the brothers and sisters, and love with faith, from God the Father and the Lord Jesus Christ. Grace be with all those who love our Lord Jesus Christ in immortality.

So ends the Letter to the Ephesians; these last few lines show why many scholars do not regard the letter as coming from the apostle himself, despite the personal references: 'love with faith' and 'grace' used in this way, as well as the odd reference to 'Jesus Christ in immortality' all sound different from Paul. Nevertheless, the author of the epistle certainly both knew and understood Paul's thinking; and I have to say that of all the Pauline corpus, it was this document that most seized me and moved me while I was doing the translation.

The Letter to the Philippians

The Letter to the Philippians

This is Paul's most joyful letter, even though it was written in a prison from which he might not emerge alive. The Philippians were perhaps his favourite community (though the Corinthians might be characteristically disposed to argue the point); they were almost the first of his foundations in Europe – see Acts 16 for the details.

Opening greetings

1 1,2 Paul and Timothy, slaves of Christ Jesus, to all the saints in Christ Jesus who are in Philippi, with the overseers and assistants, grace to you and peace from God our Father, and from the Lord Jesus Christ.

A characteristic opening from Paul and his co-worker. Not for the first time, he describes himself as 'Jesus' slave'. The words translated as 'overseers' and 'assistants' later turned into 'bishops' and 'deacons', but it is unlikely that they had that meaning at this early stage.

Thanksgiving

3-11 I give thanks to my God every time I think of you, all the time in each one of my prayers on behalf of all of you, making the prayer with joy, because of your solidarity in the gospel, from the first day until now, confident of this, that the one who started a good work in you will bring it to completion by the day of Christ Jesus, as it is [only] right for me to be thinking about all of you, because I keep you in my heart, both in my imprisonment and in the defence and establishment of the gospel, since all of you are in solidarity with me in grace.

For God is my witness that I long for all of you in the heart of Christ Jesus. And this is my prayer, that your love may overflow more and more in knowledge and in all insight, that you may test out the things that are superior, that you may be pure and blameless for Christ's Day, filled with the fruit of that righteousness that comes through Jesus Christ to the glory and praise of God.

In the thanksgiving of Pauline letters, it is always wise to look out for themes that will reappear in the rest of the letter. Three times here he uses the phrase 'all of you', which may be a sly reference to their disunity, something of which he will speak later on. Notice also the first reference to 'joy', which we shall often meet again in this letter. Though Paul is writing from prison (we cannot be sure where or when) this is nevertheless the most joy filled of all his letters. And, finally, there are various words derived from the root koinonia, *which I have translated as 'solidarity', but carries hints of partnership, union, communion, fellowship. The reader should keep all these ideas in mind when thinking about this word.*

Paul often puts some very important material into his 'thanksgivings'. What does this 'thanksgiving' tell us about his relationship to the Philippians?

And what does Paul mean when he says 'I long for all of you in the heart of Christ Jesus'?

Some of Paul's difficulties

12-17 My brothers and sisters, I want you to know that my circumstances have actually led more to the progress of the gospel, so that my imprisonment has (in Christ) become well-known among the entire praetorium, and to everyone else, and the majority of the brothers and sisters in the Lord have, because of my imprisonment, had the confidence and, increasingly, the courage to speak the word fearlessly. Some preach Christ out of envy and rivalry, while others proclaim him out of good will. Some do it for love; they know that I am put here in order to mount a defence of the gospel. While others proclaim Christ with mixed motives; they think that they will stir up trouble for me in prison.

It is quite hard to reconstruct what is going on while Paul is in prison, though presumably his Philippians knew what he was talking about; but notice his calm contemplation of the odd fact that people are actually using the gospel to upset him (and Paul is not always the calmest of souls!), and his eye for the main point, that, one way or another, the gospel gets preached.

The 'praetorium' to which Paul refers is anywhere where the local Roman governor might live, and includes also the troops that form his bodyguard.

What has Paul's imprisonment done for the gospel? Do you think that this quite often happens?

Only Christ matters

18-26 So what? But in every way, whether for false motives or true, Christ is proclaimed; and I rejoice at that.

No – but I ***shall*** rejoice. For I am sure that through your prayers and through the support of the Spirit of Jesus Christ, all this will turn out for my deliverance, according to my eager expectation and hope, that I shall in no way be ashamed; no – Christ will be glorified in my body, with all boldness, both now and always, whether by [my] life or by [my] death.

You see, for me, to live is Christ, and to die is a gain; but if continuing to live in the body means that my work will bear fruit, then I do not know which I shall choose. I am torn between the two: I have a desire to depart and be with Christ (for that is far better). On the other hand, to remain in the body is more necessary because of you; and since I am convinced of this, I know that I shall remain and stay by you all, for your own advancement and the joy of your faith, so that your boasting may overflow in Christ Jesus by means of my being present to you once more.

This is a charming passage, and reveals Paul's profound sense of the things that really matter: a) Jesus Christ; b) the proclamation of the gospel of Christ; c) the welfare of Christ's Church.

He is profoundly convinced that death would mean being once more with his beloved (and is therefore a welcome gift), but is prepared to stay with the Church despite his own preference. Notice how once again he speaks of 'you all'.

Why is Paul rejoicing here?

'To die is a gain'. Do you agree?

Faith is not easy: sporting metaphors

27-30 Just conduct your life in a way that is worthy of the gospel of Christ, so that whether I come and see you, or whether I am absent and hear all about you, [I may know] that you stand fast in one Spirit and in one mind, fighting side by side for the gospel faith, and not being intimidated in any way by your opponents; for [the faith] is a sign of destruction for them, but [a sign] of salvation for you – and [it comes] from God. Because being on Christ's side has been given as a free gift to you, not just for you to believe in him, but also to suffer for him, sharing the same struggle as you saw, and now hear about, in my case.

Paul acknowledges here that the Philippians are not having an easy time of it; but then, as he points out, neither is he. He uses various sporting metaphors ('fighting side by side', 'opponents', 'struggle'), possibly drawn from Stoic philosophy, or possibly because that was language that the Philippians easily understood.

The word 'gospel' is another important idea in Philippians: it is used twice in this section, making six times in all in Chapter 1 of the letter.

Do you think that the gospel always brings opposition with it?

Please be united

2 1-18 Therefore if there is any comfort in Christ, if there is any consolation of love, if there is any solidarity of the Spirit, if there is any compassion or pity, fill up my joy: [I want] you to think the same, have the same love, and be of one mind, with just a single thought, with no thoughts that are in line with selfish ambition or empty conceit. No – in humility, think of each other as your superiors; don't be each of you looking to your own [interests]; instead, look to each other's interests. Let your thinking be what was in Christ Jesus,

who, being in the form of God,
did not think it plunder to hang on to
(the being equal to God).
Instead, he emptied himself,
taking a slave's form,
coming to be in the likeness of human beings.
And being found in appearance like a human being,
he humbled himself!
He became obedient even to the point of death
(death on a cross!).

Therefore God superexalted him
and gave him the free gift of the name
which is above every name,
that at the name of Jesus
every knee should bow
in heaven and on earth and under the earth
and every tongue confess
that Jesus Christ is Lord
to the glory of God the Father.

So, my dear ones, just as you have always been obedient, not just when I have been present, but now all the more when I am absent, with fear and trembling work out your own salvation. For it is God who is bringing about in you the willing and the working for [God's] good will. Do everything without any muttering or argument, so that you may become blameless and innocent, unblemished children of God in the middle of a crooked and perverse generation, among whom [I want you to] appear like stars in the world. Hold on to the word of life, so as to give me something to boast about on the Day of Christ, to prove that I did not train in vain, or labour in vain. No – even if I am poured out as a sacrificial offering for your faith, I rejoice – and share my joy with all of you. In just the same way, you must rejoice – and share your joy with me.

Now we can see what we have been suspecting for a while, that Paul is addressing a problem of disunity at Philippi; his tactic is to urge them to 'think the same' as each other, but also to have the same attitude as his beloved Jesus, an attitude of not seeking to 'hang on to what you have', but of 'self-emptying', and regarding others as superior. That is how you build the 'solidarity' that for Paul was the mark of a Christian Church, as he stresses in his correspondence with the Christians of Rome, and, especially, Corinth. This tactic leads him into the 'hymn to Christ'. Whether or not it really was a hymn, and whether Paul composed it, or used existing material that was already a part of the Christian liturgy, cannot now be determined for certain, though in the translation I have followed one of the ways of setting it out as a hymn. It is a lovely passage, and has remained a favourite with Christians ever since; its theology of 'who Jesus was' is a very exalted one (at least on the most obvious way of reading it). But notice how Paul's theology is intimately linked to his pastoral concerns.

Once again, we see the words 'joy' and 'solidarity'. Reflect on why they are important to Paul in his dealings with the Philippians.

In what sense did Christ 'empty himself'?

Timothy and Epaphroditus

2 19–3 1 I hope in the Lord Jesus to send Timothy to you soon, so that I too may be
heartened by hearing about you. For I have no one who is on the same
wave-length, who genuinely cares about your interests. For they are all pursuing their

own interests, not those of Jesus Christ. But you know his quality; [you know] how he slaved at my side for the gospel, like a child with his father. So that's the one whom I'm hoping to send, immediately, as soon as I see what is going to happen to me. And I trust in the Lord that I also shall come soon.

I thought it necessary to send you Epaphroditus, my fellow Christian and co-worker and comrade-in-arms, and your apostle, and the one who has served my need; because he was longing for all of you, and was much distressed, because you had heard that he had been ill. He had indeed been ill, close to death; but God had mercy on him, and not just on him, but on me also, so that I should not have sorrow upon sorrow. So I despatched him all the more enthusiastically, so that when you saw him, you would rejoice once more, and I might have my sorrow relieved. So welcome him in the Lord with all joy; and hold people like that in honour, because it was on account of the work for Christ that he came near to death, risking his life, so that he might fill up your lack by giving service to me.

For the rest, my brothers and sisters, rejoice in the Lord. (It is no problem to me to repeat what I have written, and it is a safeguard for you.)

Paul regarded those whom he sent as equivalent to him; and in Timothy and Epaphroditus the churches may have felt they were getting 'second-best' (see 1 Corinthians 16:10,11); and the language Paul uses to commend Epaphroditus will remind the reader of how he dealt with the Corinthians in their disdain for Stephanas (1 Corinthians 16:15-18), whose Greek name may suggest that he and Epaphroditus were of a similarly lowly social status.

Once again, the word 'joy' appears (once as a noun, and twice in the verbal form, 'rejoice'). Once again, the phrase 'all of you', possibly another reference to Philippian disunity, appears.

Do you think that a snobbish preference for Paul over his emissary was the source of some of the disunity?

A sudden change of tone

2-11 Watch out for the dogs; watch out for evil workers; watch out for the 'chopping-cision' party. For ***we*** are the 'circumcision party', we who worship by the Spirit of God, and who boast in Christ Jesus, and who do not place our reliance in the flesh. Although I have reliance in the flesh also: if someone else thinks they [can] rely on the flesh, I am more capable of doing so: [I am] of the eighth-day circumcision, of the race of Israel, of the tribe of Benjamin, a Hebrew born of Hebrews, a Pharisee as regards the law, a persecutor of the Church as regards fanatical enthusiasm, I became irreproachable as regards law-righteousness.

No – whatever was on my credit-side, I regarded it as loss, because of Christ. In fact I regard everything as loss, because of the supreme good of the knowledge of Christ Jesus my Lord, for whose sake I lost everything, and I regard it as dung, in order that I may gain Christ, and take my place in him, without any righteousness of my own that comes from the law, but only the righteousness that comes through Christ's faith, the righteousness that comes from God on those who believe: so as to know him and the power of his resurrection, and solidarity with his sufferings, being conformed to his death, if somehow I may reach up to the resurrection from the dead.

> *Some scholars, observing that the beginning of Chapter 3 ('for the rest . . . ') looks like the start of the conclusion of the letter, and that suddenly the tone changes in the very next verse, have suggested that this is part of another letter. In fact, however, Paul often changes his tone rather suddenly; and in any case, the angry note does not continue throughout the section, as Paul turns to speak of God's righteousness and Paul's share in his Christ's resurrection and sufferings.*
>
> *Once again, we must be grateful to whoever it was that annoyed Paul sufficiently for him to indulge in reminiscences of his past life, which otherwise we should never have had. He indulges in a slightly cumbersome metaphor, difficult to put smoothly into English, about the 'profit' and 'loss' side of ancient accounting practice, to describe the importance of Christ to him, in comparison with what he once had.*
>
> *The reference to 'chopping-cision' in the first line of this section is a heavy attempt to reproduce Paul's somewhat offensive pun on 'circumcision'.*
>
> *Is there anything that* **you** *would be reluctant to let go of for the sake of Jesus Christ?*

A sporting metaphor

12-14 Not that I've already received the gold medal, or reached perfection, but I'm in pursuit of it, in the hope of winning it, seeing that I've been won by Christ Jesus. My fellow Christians, I do not reckon that I have won: but one thing [I do]. Forgetting the previous laps, I am pushing towards those which lie ahead, in pursuit of the finishing line, towards the medal, which consists in the summons [that comes] from God in Jesus Christ, [to go] higher.

> *We may find that the awkwardness of this metaphor conveys at one and the same time Paul's determination to catch his readers' attention by using an image from the athletics field, and his own lack of familiarity with the sport. Or, more prosaically, the image may have come to him by way of Stoic philosophy, which seems to have been a part of his cultural baggage. It would be pushing a harmless metaphor too far if we started asking whether the analogy with training for a sport does not signal a return to 'righteousness by works'!*

Christ should make a difference to the way we behave

3 15–4 1 So those who are 'perfect', let us keep thinking this way; and if your thoughts are different in some way, God will reveal this also to you – only [we should] hold to whatever we have attained.

Join [with the others] in following my example, brothers and sisters; keep an eye on those who are behaving like us, whom you have as your model. For many people are behaving – whom I have mentioned to you, and now I am in tears as I mention them

– [as] enemies of the cross of Christ, whose end is destruction, whose god is their belly, and whose glory is their shame, those whose thoughts are earthbound. For our country is in heaven, from which we are waiting for a saviour, the Lord Jesus Christ, who will transform our humble body, conforming it to his glorious body, according to his power which enables him to subordinate everything to him. So, my beloved and longed-for brothers and sisters, my joy and my crown, stand firm like this in the Lord, beloved.

Paul is never shy about offering himself as an example. The encounter with Christ had transformed his life, made a visible difference. He is quite clear about the kind of behaviour that is appropriate for Christians, and that which is not.

Occasionally, in his enthusiasm, the syntax falls apart; or perhaps his secretary could not keep up with his dictation! One example would be the sentence beginning 'For many people are behaving . . .'

'Our country is in heaven'. What does this mean to you?

Stop quarrelling

2,3 I beg Evodia, and I beg Syntyche to think the same in the Lord. Yes, and I ask you too, my true partner, give them help; for these women have fought side by side with me in the arena of the gospel, and also with Clemens, and the rest of my fellow-workers, whose names are in the book of life.

We have on several occasions in the letter so far seen possible hints of disunity at Philippi, often in connection with the word 'thinking' (see Philippians 1.7; 2:2; 2:5; 3:15; 3:19; 4:10); here we see a clear instance, where named people are causing scandal in the body. The word translated as 'partner' (for which the Greek is Syzygos*) is thought by at least one eminent scholar to refer to Paul's wife. It is certainly a thought-provoking possibility, although it is also just possible that* Syzygos *is a personal name.*

Do Christians often fight?

Peace and joy

4-9 Rejoice at all times in the Lord; again I shall say [it]: rejoice! Let your decency be known to all people. The Lord is near: don't be anxious about anything, but in all your prayer and intercession, with thanksgiving let your requests be known to God; and the peace of God which is beyond all imagining will guard your hearts and your minds in Christ Jesus.

For the rest, brothers and sisters, whatever is true, whatever is honourable, whatever is righteous, whatever is holy, whatever is agreeable, whatever is attractive, anything that is virtue or praise – think of these things.

And whatever you have learnt and received and heard and seen in me – do these things.

And the God of peace will be with you.

Again the letter seems to be coming to a close; it's a lovely passage, which starts with our familiar 'rejoice', and focuses the Philippians on God, on prayer, and, in a few charming lines, on all that it is proper for us to think of and all that we should do. Then there is what sounds like the beginning of a Pauline farewell: 'the God of peace will be with you'. But there is more to come.

Have you ever experienced this 'peace of God which is beyond all imagining'? When?

The gift Epaphroditus brought to Paul

10-20 I rejoiced greatly in the Lord that already, some time ago, you had revived your [habit of] thinking about me (insofar as you were thinking about me, but you lacked the opportunity). Not that I am talking because of any need: for I have learnt how to be content, where I am. I know how to be humbled, and I know how to have enough and to spare. In everything and in every respect I am an expert: being satisfied and being hungry; being in surplus and being in want. In every respect I am strong in the one who empowers me.

Nevertheless, it was a lovely thing that you did, when you showed me solidarity in my trouble. You too know, Philippians, that in the beginning of the gospel, when I came out of Macedonia, no church showed me any solidarity of debit and credit, except for you people alone; because even in Thessalonica, on two or three occasions, you sent me something towards my needs. Not that I am fishing for the gift; what I am fishing for is the profit that increases to the settlement of your account. I have received payment in full, and I have enough and to spare. I am fully supplied, having received your contribution from Epaphroditus, an odour of fragrance, an acceptable sacrifice, pleasing to God.

My God will fill up all your need, according to his wealth in glory in Christ Jesus: to our God and Father be the glory, for ever and ever. Amen.

Notice the familiar words 'rejoice' and 'think'. Clearly the Philippians have, in the past and more recently, been generous in their contributions to Paul, but perhaps he is in need again. As always with Paul, everything begins and ends with Christ.

Once again he uses the fiscal metaphor of 'debit and credit', and it bumps along, a little uncomfortably. He is more at ease when he turns to an image from the Old Testament cult: 'an odour of fragrance, an acceptable sacrifice'.

Do you think that Paul is at all mercenary?

Closing greetings

21-23 Greet every single saint in Christ Jesus. The brothers and sisters who are with me send greetings; all the saints send you greetings, especially those from Caesar's household.

The grace of our Lord Jesus Christ be with the spirit of you [all].

The closing greetings have fewer names than in other Pauline epistles; the reference to 'Caesar's household' may be a reminder to his hearers or readers that Paul is not a complete failure as an evangelist!

The Letter to the Colossians

The Letter to the Colossians

This is a lovely letter, perhaps written by Paul towards the end of his life, or by someone else (Timothy?) under Paul's instruction, or shortly after his death, to let third- and fourth-generation Christians know 'this is what Paul is saying to us today'. Colossae is about a hundred miles east of Ephesus, and quite near Laodicea (whose church is mentioned in Chapter 4). There are connections with the letter to Philemon; see the references in Chapter 4 to Epaphras, Luke, Aristarchus, Onesimus and Demas.

Opening greetings

1 1, 2 Paul, an apostle of Christ Jesus through the will of God, and Timothy [our] fellow Christian, to the saints at Colossae, faithful brothers and sisters in Christ, grace to you and peace, from God our Father.

This is a standard opening to a Pauline letter, whether or not Paul wrote it.

Thanksgiving

3-8 We give thanks to God, [the] Father of our Lord Jesus Christ, all the time, when we pray for you, having heard of your faith in Christ Jesus, and the love which you have for all the saints, on account of the hope which is laid up for you in heaven, which you heard about before, in the word of truth of the gospel which has come to you, just as it is bearing fruit and growing in the whole world, so also in you, from the day when you heard and recognised the grace of God in truth, as you learnt from Epaphras, our beloved fellow slave, who is a faithful minister of Christ for you, who told us about your love in the Spirit.

This thanksgiving is a single sentence in Greek, and we have left it so in English, at some cost, perhaps, to the reader's patience; you are advised to take it gently, and count the number of different things for which the author is thanking God. Like Ephesians, but to nowhere near the same extent, we have in this letter a frequent piling-up of nouns, such as 'the word of truth of the gospel', for example.

What is Paul thanking God for in this section?

The author's prayer

9-14 Because of this, we also, from the day when we [first] heard, do not cease praying for you, and asking that you may be filled with the knowledge of his will in all wisdom and spiritual understanding, to walk worthily of the Lord, to please him in all things, bearing fruit and growing in every good work, through the knowledge of God, being empowered with all power, according to the might of his glory, with a view to all patience and fortitude.

Joyfully giving thanks to the Father who made us fit for the portion of the lot of the saints in light, who delivered us from the authority of darkness and changed us into the kingdom of the Son of his love, in whom we have redemption, the forgiveness of sins.

Some scholars think of these verses as part of the thanksgiving, but it seems easier to read it as the author's prayer for his hearers or readers. The attentive reader will notice that the phrase 'bearing fruit and growing' makes its second appearance in the letter. The first time, it refers to the spread of the gospel; on the second occasion, it is something that is desired for the Christians of Colossae. Possibly it is something that, in the author's view, they lack.

'That you may be filled with the knowledge of his will'. Why does Paul make this prayer for the Colossians? Would his prayer for you be the same?

The hymn to Christ

15-20 [He] is the icon of the invisible God,
the first-born of all creation.
Because in him all was created,
in heaven and on earth,
what is visible or invisible:
whether thrones or lordships,
whether rules or authorities,
through him and for him was all created.
And he is before all,
and all has come to exist in him.
And he is the head of the body, the Church;
[he] is the beginning, first-born from the dead,
that he himself might become Number One in all.
Because in him all the Fullness was pleased to dwell
and through him to reconcile all to him,
having made peace through the blood of his cross
through him, whether the things on earth or the things in heaven.

This is an extraordinary piece of writing, and scholars have not fully agreed on what it is. Often, though, it is described as a hymn to Christ, perhaps one already in use in the liturgy at Colossae, to which the author has added some elements in order to make a theological point. As it stands, it sings about Christ as 'Number One', in creation, and in redemption. Some scholars see it as a meditation on the opening words of the Bible, 'In the beginning, God created the heavens and the earth'.

'In him all the Fullness was pleased to dwell': what do you think this might mean?

What Christ has done for the readers

21-23 And you, who were once alienated, and enemies in your mind, because of wicked works, now he has reconciled [you] by the body of his flesh, through death, to offer you as holy and blameless and irreproachable before him – as long as you remain established and steadfast in the faith, not shifting from the hope of the gospel you heard, which was proclaimed in all creation under heaven, of which I, Paul, became a minister.

Many scholars regard this as the summary of the message of Colossians, a statement of what Christ has done for Paul's addressees, and an indication of what their response might be.

What Paul is doing for his people

1[24]–2[5] Now I rejoice in my sufferings on your behalf; and I fill up what is lacking in the affliction of Christ-in-my-flesh, on behalf of his Body, which is the Church,

- of which I became a servant according to God's arrangement,
- which was given me for you, to bring God's word to completion,
- the mystery that was hidden from the ages and from the generations
- but now has been revealed to his saints,
- to whom God wished to make known what is the wealth of the glory of this mystery among the Gentiles,
- which is Christ among you, the hope of glory,
- whom we proclaim, admonishing everybody, and teaching everybody in all wisdom,
- that we may present everybody as perfect in Christ – that is the goal towards which I am labouring,
- struggling in accordance with his action that is active in me in power.

For I want you to know what a huge struggle I have, for you and for those in Laodicea, and those who have not physically seen my face, so that their hearts may be comforted, united by love, and for them to have all wealth of the assurance of understanding, and [for them to have] the knowledge of the mystery of God, Christ, in whom all the treasures of wisdom and knowledge are hidden.

This is what I am saying: let no one fool you by plausible arguments. For even if I am physically absent, nevertheless I am with you in spirit, rejoicing as I look at your orderliness, and the firmness of your faith in Christ.

As so often in Ephesians, here we have a long and slightly unwieldy sentence, whose structure I have tried to show by means of bullet points. As so often in Paul's genuine letters, theology and pastoral practice walk closely together, hand in hand.

'I fill up what is lacking in the affliction of Christ-in-my-flesh': what do you think this means?

Be confident in the gospel of the Resurrection

6-15 So, as you have received Christ Jesus as Lord, walk in him, rooted in him and built on him and established in the faith, as you have been taught, overflowing in gratitude.

Watch out that someone does not take you prisoner through philosophy and empty falsehood,

- according to the tradition of human beings, according to the elementals of the universe, and not according to Christ,
- because in Christ dwells all the fullness of divinity, in bodily form, and you are fulfilled in him,
- who is the head of all rule and authority
- in whom also you have been circumcised, with a circumcision not made by hands, by the stripping off of the body of flesh, by Christ's circumcision, being buried with him in baptism
- in which you have also been raised through faith in the activity of God, who raised him from the dead.

And you, who were dead because of [your] transgressions, he made you alive along with him, freely forgiving us all our transgressions, wiping out the written evidence against us, the bond, and its requirements, which was opposed to us – and he took it out of the field of play, nailing it to the Cross, stripping off the rules and authorities, he made a public example of them, confidently holding a triumph over them in it.

Another long sentence holds together the warning against alternative doctrines and the reaffirmation of the gospel tradition. The author here reminds his hearers or readers of the tradition that they have received, and of their absolute grounds for confidence in Jesus, in his divinity, his resurrection, and his conquest of everything that threatened them.

The phrase that I have translated 'rule and authority' appears frequently in Colossians and in the Pastoral Letters. The author here uses metaphors from moneylending ('the bond'), sport ('the field of play') and Roman military parades ('triumph') to underline the completeness of God's victory over the 'authorities'.

The Colossians are told to 'watch out that someone does not take you prisoner through philosophy, and empty falsehood'. What might the author warn us against today?

Warning against following false teachings

16-23 So let no one pass judgement on you with regard to food and drink, or in respect to a festival, or new moon or Sabbath. These things are [merely] shadows of what is to come – the reality belongs to Christ. Don't let anyone cheat you of your prize, through insisting on self-abasement and angel-worship, entering upon [a description of] what they have seen, foolishly puffed up by their fleshly mind, and not holding on to the head, from whom the whole body is supported and held together by sinews and ligaments, and will grow the growth of God.

If you have died with Christ and [are liberated] from the elements of the world, why let yourselves be dictated to, as though you were still living in the world? 'Don't handle; don't taste; don't touch.' These things are all heading for destruction by wear and tear, in keeping human commandments and teachings; they have a rhetoric of cleverness with their self-chosen worship and humiliation, and their severity on the body, with no value against the indulgence of the flesh.

Scholars have made valiant, and mutually contradictory, attempts to establish what the false teaching might have been, though certainly the Colossians will have known what Paul was talking about. Rather than pry any deeper into these murky thickets, the reader should make for what really interests the author; for him, the prime concern is to not let go of death-with-Christ and rising-with-Christ. Nothing else matters.

The phrases 'destruction by wear and tear' and 'with no value against the indulgence of the flesh' more or less accurately translate the Greek, but it is not absolutely clear what the author is getting at. This is because we really do not know what the 'false philosophy' was; but the basic point seems to be that the practices into which the Colossians are being seduced are merely human, and therefore transitory, and, although aimed at restricting self-indulgence, will turn out to be ineffective.

The Colossians are warned to 'hold on to the head'. What does this mean for us today? What shadowy religious ideas might distract today's Christians from the solid reality of the faith?

How to live in Christ

3 1-17 So, if you have been raised with Christ, seek the things that are above, where Christ is seated at God's right hand;

- think of the things that are above, not of things on earth.
- For you have died, and your life is hidden with Christ in God.
- When Christ appears, [who is] your life, then also you will appear with him in glory.
- So put to death your earthly parts: fornication, impurity, passion, evil desire, and greed (which is idolatry);
- through these things the anger of God is coming on the children of disobedience;
- among them you once walked, because you lived among them;
- now, however, you have also put everything aside: anger, rage, evil, blasphemy, filthy talk from your mouth;
- don't tell lies to others,
- having put off the old person, with all its practices, and

- having put on the new person who is made new in knowledge, in accordance with the likeness of the one who created him,
- where there is no 'Greek and Jew', 'circumcision and uncircumcision', 'barbarian', 'Scythian', 'slave', 'free',
- but Christ is all in all.

So, as God's chosen ones, holy and beloved ones, put on new clothes: merciful compassion, goodness, humility, gentleness, patience, putting up with each other, and forgiving each other, if anyone has a complaint against another: as the Lord forgave you, so you must also do.

On top of all these, [put on] love, which is the bond that unites perfectly. And may Christ's love referee in your hearts, to which you were called in one body – and become grateful!

Let Christ's word live richly in you, teaching and admonishing yourselves in all wisdom, with psalms, hymns, spiritual canticles, singing with thanks in your hearts to God. And everything that you do, in deed or word, do everything in the Lord Jesus' name, giving thanks to God the Father through him.

It is a consistent theme in the Pauline letters, both those that are clearly from the apostle's hand, and those that may have come from later disciples, that being a follower of Christ makes a visible difference. The basic attitude is 'upwards', a heart set on God; and that means that some kinds of behaviour are ruled out, while others are expected. Another consistent theme is that what God has done in Christ means that there is no room for artificial distinctions, racial, religious, or social. All that matters is Christ, who is mentioned no less than six times in these verses.

The Scythians were a group from modern Russia, of notorious crudeness and cruelty. The point is that no one is excluded from the mystery of God-in-Christ, no matter who they are or what they have done.

The reference to Christ as 'referee' translates a word that means to 'umpire' in the Games, such as the Olympics, where the function of the umpire was a great deal more unchallenged than in their modern equivalent. The point is the absolute completeness of Christ's (peace-giving) command over the Christian.

In what sense is greed 'idolatry'?

The 'household code'

3[18–]4[1]

- ***Wives*** – be subject to your husbands, as is proper in the Lord.
- ***Husbands*** – love your wives, and don't get embittered against them.
- ***Children*** – obey your parents in every respect; for this is pleasing in the Lord.
- ***Fathers*** – don't irritate your children, so that they don't get dispirited.

- ***Slaves*** – in every respect, obey those who are your 'lords' according to the flesh, not in 'serving to attract attention', like those who try to please human beings, but in simplicity of heart, fearing the ***Lord***. Whatever you do, work from the heart, as for the ***Lord***, and not for human beings, knowing that [it is] from the ***Lord*** [that] you will receive the reward of the inheritance. Be slaves to ***the Lord Christ***. For the one who does what is unrighteous gets the reward of the unrighteousness he has done – and there is no snobbery.
- '***Lords***' – give what is righteous and fair to your 'slaves', knowing that you also have a '***Lord***' in heaven.

At first reading, this passage gives us a bit of a shock, for it seems to undo the sense of equality of all Christians before the Lord; but notice how the author relativises what looks like rampant hierarchy. It is true that wives and children and slaves are told to keep their places, but so are husbands, fathers, and slave-lords. And look at the last pairing – see how much longer is the section given to slaves, and how the wordplay between 'slave-lord' and 'Lord' puts all human rankings into perspective. Though it is sadly true that some Christians have read this text in such a way as to justify exploitation and subordination, it simply means that they have not looked attentively enough at it.

How should we apply these teachings to our own situation?

Final instructions

2-6 Be persistent in prayer; be wide awake about it, in gratitude; at the same time, pray for us, that God may open for us a door for the word, to speak of the mystery of Christ, for which I am in prison, so that I may make it plain, as I must speak. Behave 'cleverly' towards outsiders; make the most of the time. Let your speech always be agreeable, seasoned with salt, to know how you must answer each one.

The obligation to pray for one another is frequently stressed in Paul, as is the eagerness for mission, and the emphasis on Christ (as well as the connection between being an apostle and being in prison). Paul nearly always stresses the importance of correct relations with outsiders.

What does 'behave "cleverly" towards outsiders' mean?

Final greetings

7-18 Tychicus, beloved fellow Christian, faithful servant, and fellow slave in the Lord, will tell you all about me; I am sending him to you for that precise purpose, that you may know about us, and he may comfort your hearts, along with Onesimus, a faithful and much-loved fellow Christian, who is one of you. They'll inform you of everything at this end.

Aristarchus, my fellow prisoner, greets you, as does Mark, Barnabas's cousin (about whom you have received instructions; if he comes to you, give him hospitality), and

Jesus (the one called 'Justus'), who are [all] of the Circumcision; these alone are my fellow workers to [build up] the kingdom of God, and have been a comfort to me.

Epaphras greets you, who is one of you and a slave of Jesus Christ, who is all the time fighting on your behalf in his prayers, that you may stand perfect and fully assured in all that God wills. I can testify to him, that he has much hard labour on your behalf, and also on behalf of those in Laodicea and Hierapolis. Luke the beloved doctor greets you all, as does Demas.

Greet the brothers and sisters in Laodicea, and Nympha and the church that meets at her house; and when this letter has been read among you, make arrangements for it to be read in the church of the Laodiceans; and I want you also to read the one from Laodicea. And tell Archippus, 'Watch out for the ministry that you have received in the Lord; make sure that you fulfil it.'

The greeting in my hand: PAUL. REMEMBER MY CHAINS.

Grace be with you.

The list of names, including that of Onesimus, makes a clear link between the letters to the Colossians and to Philemon. Indeed some scholars suspect that the rather sharp-sounding reminder to Archippus to 'watch out for the ministry' may be addressed to the actual addressee of Philemon, and may refer to Paul's demand that he set Onesimus free. Notice how the author commends his various fellow workers, to give them standing in both Colossae and Laodicea (the letter is to be read in both places). Titles like 'fellow slave', 'fellow captive', 'slave of Christ Jesus', 'beloved doctor', and adjectives like 'faithful' and 'beloved', all tend in that direction. Certainly something like the message to Archippus, whether or not it is about freeing Onesimus, makes it harder to imagine that the letter is entirely pseudonymous. Recently a strong case has been made for Timothy having written Colossians, under Paul's supervision; and that is entirely possible.

What sense do you get of the relationship between Paul and his apostolic co-workers?

The First Letter to the Thessalonians

The First Letter to the Thessalonians

In the view of many scholars, this is the first of Paul's letters, in which case the opening verse contains the first words of the New Testament to have been written. (If you find yourself puzzling about why, in that case, this letter is positioned so late in the collection of Paul's letters, the answer is quite simple: they are collected in order of their length!) We should read them in awed tones.

We share with Paul and his readers the problem of living our Christianity in a hostile and pagan culture.

Opening greeting

1 1 Paul and Silvanus and Timothy to the Church of the Thessalonians in God the Father and the Lord Jesus Christ, grace to you and peace.

It may be worth looking at a map to see where Thessalonica is, and at Acts 16, to see how Paul came to found the Church there. This first document of the New Testament apparently has three authors (but outside of this opening verse you would hardly know that Silvanus and Timothy are involved). Notice that Paul thinks of 'God the Father' and 'the Lord Jesus Christ' as practically the same.

The thanksgiving

2-10 We give thanks to God for all of you, always making mention of you in our prayers, remembering your work of faith and the labour of love, and the perseverance of hope of our Lord Jesus Christ in the presence of our God and Father, knowing as we do, beloved brothers and sisters, the fact that you have been chosen, because our gospel did not come to you just in rhetoric, but also in power and in the Holy Spirit, and with full conviction, as you know the kind of people we were among you for your sake.

And you became imitators of us and of the Lord, welcoming the message in considerable affliction, and with joy in the Holy Spirit, so that you became a model to all the believers in Macedonia, and in Achaia as well. For from you the Lord's word has sounded forth, not just in Macedonia and Achaia, but in every place your faith in God has gone out, so that we have no need to say anything. For it is they who report about us what kind of a welcome we had from you, and how you turned to God from idols, to become slaves of the living and true God, and to wait for his Son [coming] from heaven, whom he raised from the dead, Jesus, who delivers us from the wrath that is coming.

Letters in the ancient world tended to have a thanksgiving, after the introduction, and Paul follows that pattern. In the thanksgiving of his letters, which are rather longer than other letters of his time, we find that he plays out the themes that will appear again in the letter. Such themes might include, in this case, the fact of waiting for Jesus to return, and the belief that Jesus 'delivers us from the wrath that is coming'. In addition, notice the teaching, so central to Paul's theology, that God raised Jesus from the dead. Note, too, the word 'Lord', which appears three times in Chapter 1. To whom does it refer? The Holy Spirit appears twice; we also have the mention of the three virtues of faith, love and hope, which will reappear in a different form in 1 Corinthians 13.

Three other points will be useful to notice at this stage: First, the Thessalonian Christians had obviously come from paganism (the reference to idols would have been impossible if they had been Jews). Second, Jesus is 'Son of God'. This is very familiar to us now; but what does Paul mean by it? Who is Jesus for Paul? Third, notice that the opening section of this sentence is very long, and has a string of nouns ('labour of love', 'perseverance of hope of our Lord'), so the appearance of a string of nouns does not mean that Paul did not write a particular passage.

What does it mean to say that Jesus 'delivers us from the wrath that is coming'?

Paul's arrival at Thessalonica

2 1-4 For you yourselves know, brothers and sisters, about our arrival with you, and that it was not useless. No – although we had, as you know, previously experienced suffering and insults at Philippi, we had full confidence in our God to speak the gospel of God to you amid strong opposition. You see, our comfort is not from deception or impure motives or by trickery. No – as we have been found worthy by God to be entrusted with the gospel, so we speak, not pleasing human beings, but pleasing God who tests our hearts.

Paul starts with what is common ground between him and his Thessalonians. The word 'useless' (literally 'empty') is a frequent concern in his later letters, as is his emphasis on suffering and opposition for the sake of the 'gospel'. The word 'gospel' is worth watching, to see how Paul uses it. Absolutely at the heart of Paul's self-consciousness is his certainty that he is called by God to proclaim the gospel, and his insistence that he does it with integrity.

The reader must decide whether 'our comfort', of which Paul speaks, is the comfort he gives or the comfort he receives.

Paul speaks of 'strong opposition': is this inevitable for those who preach the gospel?

How Paul preached in Thessalonica

5-12 For, as you know, it was not with any verbal flattery, nor, as God is my witness, through concealed greed, nor with an eye on honour from human beings, whether from you or from any other people; we can wield authority as apostles of Christ. We, however, became like infants in the midst of you, just as a nursing mother cherishes her children, so in our longing for you we were determined to share with you, not merely the gospel of God, but also our own selves, because you had become dear to us.

For remember, brothers and sisters, our labour and our toil; night and day we worked so as not to be a burden for any of you, and we proclaimed the gospel of God. You and God are our witnesses that we behaved to you who believe in a holy and righteous and blameless manner; as you know, we comforted each of you as a father comforts his own children, and consoled you, and testified before you, so that you should behave worthily of the God who calls you into his own kingdom and glory.

Twice in this passage Paul calls God to witness; twice he speaks of the 'gospel of God'; twice he likens himself to a parent in his dealings with the Church he has evangelised. These are aspects of Paul's attitude to his mission that surface again and again in his letters. Also present is just a touch of boastfulness, something that can be found elsewhere in Paul.

Why does Paul remind the Thessalonians of his 'labour and toil'?

How the Thessalonians responded

13-16 And because of this we give thanks to God unceasingly, because when you received the 'word of hearing' from us, you accepted it from God, not just a 'word of human beings'; no – as it really is [you accepted it] as a 'word of God', who is active among you who believe. For, my brothers and sisters, you became just like the churches of God which are in Judaea and in Christ Jesus, because you also suffered from your own fellow countrymen, precisely as they did from the Jews, who had killed both the Lord Jesus and the prophets, who chased us out, who do not please God, and are hostile to all humanity, who prevent us from talking to the Gentiles in order that they might be saved, so that they all the time fill up the measure of their sins; but the wrath has come upon them to the full.

Paul is cross here (not for the last time in his letters), but not with his correspondents, who had clearly accepted his teaching unexpectedly well. Then, in a long and slightly lost sentence, he compares them to Christians in Judaea, who have likewise endured persecution; then the sentence turns into an assault on his fellow Jews, which reads uncomfortably to us. Paul's anger, however, is the kind that can surface 'within the family'. This passage is not often read in church!

What does Paul mean by the 'wrath that has come upon' his opponents?

Paul wants to see the Thessalonians

17-20 We, however, brothers and sisters, separated from you for a brief while (in person, but ***not*** in our hearts), were more eager than ever, with a passionate longing to see your faces, because we intended to come to you, ***I, Paul***, on two or three occasions; and Satan thwarted us. For what is our hope, or our joy, or the crown of which we boast before our Lord at his coming – is it not you? For you are our glory and our joy.

Overcoming absence by a token of presence is what a letter is all about; and Paul is showing a new way for Christians to be Christian (something that you cannot do without others) in this first surviving Christian letter. Paul's love for the Thessalonians is neither forced nor exclusive; that same love can be seen in all his letters, even to the vacillating Galatians and the intractable Corinthians.

'You are our glory and our joy.' Why do you think Paul says this to the Thessalonians?

Why Timothy was sent

3 1-5 Therefore, since we could not bear it any longer, we decided it was best to be left alone in Athens; and we sent Timothy, our fellow Christian and co-worker of God in the gospel of Christ, to make you resolute and to counsel you about your faith, [so as] not to be agitated in any way in all these troubles. For you yourselves know that we are destined for this. For when we were with you, we predicted to you that we were about to be persecuted, and it turned out that way, as you know. For that reason, I sent to find out about your faith (I couldn't bear it any longer), we didn't want the Tempter to tempt you, for then perhaps our labour would be made useless.

Paul's evident affection for the Thessalonians continues; but it is possible that they thought he was giving them 'second-best' by sending Timothy, not coming himself. Certainly that was how the Corinthians were to feel later on. Notice that Paul takes it for granted that where the gospel is preached there will be persecution, and that it will put some Christians off.

Does it put **you** *off?*

Timothy's report

6-10 But Timothy came to us recently from you, and he gave us the good news about your faith and love, and that you make continuous mention of us, longing to see us, just as we long to see you; on this account we were comforted, brothers and sisters, about you, in all our distress and trouble, through your faith, because now we continue to live, if you stand firm in the Lord. For what thanksgiving can we return to the Lord for you, in all the joy with which we rejoice before our God, day and night begging most earnestly to see your face, and to make good what is lacking in your faith?

Once more, Paul's affection for the Thessalonians is unmistakable, and his desire to praise them. It seems that he was anxious about whether their faith would survive the pressure of his absence; Timothy has reassured him. Just as Christians cannot be Christians on their own, so wandering apostles need a combination of letters, agents and personal contact.

This letter powerfully expresses Paul's love for Christians in other places. Should Christians be doing the same today, and if so, how?

A prayer for the Thessalonians

11-13 May Our God and Father himself, and our Lord Jesus, straighten our road to you. May the Lord make you rich and overflowing in love to each other and to all, just as we do to you, to confirm your hearts as blameless in holiness before our God and Father at the coming of our Lord Jesus with all his saints. Amen.

> *This is a charming and affectionate prayer, and perhaps a subtle reminder to the Thessalonians that they still have a way to go. The reader might ask what it means for a good monotheist Jew like Paul to call Jesus 'Lord', and to place him as closely as he does here with 'God and Father'. Jesus is not quite identical with 'God and Father', of course, but there is a certain 'unity of action'. Notice, too, the reference to Jesus' 'coming' (Greek* parousia*), an idea which is more prominent in 1 Thessalonians than in other Pauline letters.*

Keeping the traditions and observing sexual purity

4 1-8 For the rest, brothers and sisters, we ask and beg you in the Lord Jesus, that as you received from us how you should behave and, please God, as in fact you are behaving, that you do so even better. For you know what promises we gave you through the Lord Jesus.

For this is the will of God, your sanctification, that you should abstain from fornication, that each of you should know how to keep his own vessel in holiness and honour, not in undergoing passion, like the Gentiles who do not know God, [so as] not to transgress and take advantage of one's fellow Christian in the matter, because the Lord is the one who exacts punishment for all these things, as we told you before and solemnly testified [to you]. For God did not call us to impurity but in holiness. Consequently anyone who disregards this is not disregarding human beings but God, who also gives his Holy Spirit for you.

> *Paul frequently uses language about 'receiving' and 'passing down', that refers to the traditions that he has given to his churches. For Paul, they could not pick and choose what to believe. And one problem he always had with converts who had not been brought up in the strict morality of Judaism was that they tended to ignore rules about sexual behaviour. For Paul, sexuality was too important to mess about with, and misuse of sexuality incompatible with the holiness to which they were called.*
>
> *'Keeping one's own vessel in holiness' might refer to one's body or one's wife; scholars are not agreed.*
>
> *Lastly, notice the use of the Holy Spirit, slightly less frequent in 1 Thessalonians than in other letters (see 1:5; 1:6; 5:19), but still clearly something that they could experience and feel.*
>
> *What restrictions should Christians place on their sexual activity?*

Relations within the community and without

9-12 About your love of fellow Christians, you have no need for me to write to you, for you are taught by God to love each other; for this is what you do to all the Christians in the whole of Macedonia. We beg you, fellow Christians, to be even more generous and to have it as your ambition to live in peace, to do your own thing, and to work with your own hands, just as we directed you, that you may behave decently towards outsiders, and have no need of anybody.

Sometimes, when a group is under external pressure, as the Thessalonians were, it is tempting for them to retreat behind a barrier, and to exclude the outside world from their considerations. Paul is not prepared to allow his Christians to operate in this way, in two respects. First, they must be generous to fellow Christians; very possibly he is talking here about the 'collection', so very much a concern of his and in regard to which he was later to boast to the (relatively wealthy) Corinthians of the generosity of Macedonia (1 Corinthians 8:1-7). Second, this group is to 'behave decently towards outsiders', and to work with their own hands.

Is it ever possible for Christians to be too involved in secular society?

What about Christians who have died?

13-18 About those who have fallen asleep, we want you to know, brothers and sisters; we do not want you to grieve, like those others who have no hope. For if we believe that Jesus died and rose again, so also God will bring with him those who have fallen asleep through Jesus. For this is our statement, on the basis of a word of the Lord, that we who are alive, who survive till the Lord's coming, will not have any advantage at all over those who have fallen asleep. For the Lord himself, at a word of command, at the sound of an archangel and at the trumpet of God, will come down from heaven; and the dead-in-Christ shall be raised first, then we who are alive, who survive, will be snatched up together with them in the clouds to meet the Lord in the air; and so we shall be all the time with the Lord. So comfort each other with these words.

At the heart of Paul's gospel is his faith in the Resurrection; it looks also as though he believed in a fairly imminent coming of Jesus. This, of course, raises the question as to whether or not those who are still alive when Christ comes have somehow won the race against those who have died (and some Christians must have died between the bringing of the gospel to Thessalonica and the writing of this letter). To answer this, Paul uses some symbols from Jewish speculation about the end-time. The main thing is not to worry; and that is not because of any pious fiction, but because of what Paul and his Thessalonians know God has done in Christ.

What is ***your*** *attitude to the fate of those who have died?*

Waiting for the unknown Day

5 1-11 About dates and times, brothers and sisters, you have no need of anything in writing to you. For you know precisely that the Day of the Lord is coming, just like a burglar at night. When they say 'peace and security', then a sudden destruction looms over them, as the labour pains come on a pregnant woman; and no way are they going to escape. But you, brothers and sisters, are not in darkness, that the day should come upon you like a burglar. For you are all children of light and

children of day. We do not belong to night or to darkness. So let us not sleep, then, like the rest; no – let's stay awake and be sober. For people who sleep, sleep at night, and those who get drunk, get drunk at night. We, however, who belong to the Day, are sober; we put on the breastplate of faith and love, and the helmet of faith in salvation. Because God did not put us [here] for wrath, but for obtaining salvation through our Lord Jesus Christ, who died for us, so that whether we are awake or asleep we may be alive with him. Therefore comfort each other and build each other up, just as you are doing.

Paul clearly believes that Jesus will return; but life has to continue, and he will not allow them to speculate about when this might happen. What matters is their attitude, not their watching of the cosmic clock. God's visitation is always at an unexpected time; the essential thing is to remain 'on-side', on the team of light and day, to be awake and clear-headed, and confident in what God has done in Christ.

What does Paul mean by 'the Day'?

Respect for church leaders

12, 13 We ask you, brothers and sisters, to acknowledge those who labour among you, and are appointed over you in the Lord, and who admonish you, and to have immense regard for them, because of their function. Live at peace with each other.

In Christianity, all are equal before God; but in the history of Christianity it has always been found necessary to have leaders, whatever they were called, for the stability of the group. It has also always been the case that Christians are sinful and squabbling, including, of course, sniping at church leaders. Hence the admonition to 'live at peace'. It is not that church structures are there to be worshipped, simply that they are necessary, human nature being what it is.

Are you too critical of church leaders? Or too docile towards them?

How to behave in the Body of Christ

14-22 We beg you, brothers and sisters, admonish the undisciplined, console the faint-hearted, pay attention to those who are sick, be patient with everybody. See that no one returns evil for evil to anybody. Instead, always keep going for what is good for each other and for all.

Rejoice always.
Pray without ceasing.
In everything give thanks
(for this is the will of God in Christ Jesus for you).
Do not extinguish the Spirit.
Do not despise prophecy,
but test everything (hold fast to what is good).
From every form of evil – keep away!

It is interesting for us at this distance to see what are the fundamental moral requirements, as far as Paul is concerned. There must be good order and compassion, respect for all and joy (a word frequently on Paul's lips), prayer and gratitude, and, above all, the Spirit. That means, at least sometimes, the gift of prophecy; but, as Christians have always known, it is necessary to test the spirits.

How do you and your church (if you have one) match up to the teaching of this passage? Be honest.

Concluding prayer and greetings

23-28 May the God of peace himself sanctify you through and through; and may your spirit be preserved undamaged and your body irreproachable at the coming of our Lord Jesus Christ.

The One who calls you is faithful – he will also perform!
Brothers and sisters, pray for us.
Greet all the brothers and sisters with a holy kiss.
I adjure you by the Lord to have the letter read to all the Christians.
The grace of our Lord Jesus be with you all.

So ends our earliest surviving New Testament document. Perhaps Paul, as he does elsewhere, has seized the pen, two lines from the end, and speaks of 'I' instead of 'we'. The farewell conveys his sense of absolute dependence on God, on the love that Christians should have for one another, of their mutual support in prayer, and of the physical means of building community, the 'holy kiss' and the exchange of letters. All, however, goes back to God, 'the One who . . . is faithful', and to 'the grace of our Lord Jesus Christ'.

The Second Letter to the Thessalonians

The Second Letter to the Thessalonians

Opening greetings

1 1,2 Paul and Silvanus and Timothy, to the Church of the Thessalonians in God our Father and the Lord Jesus Christ, grace to you and peace from God our Father and the Lord Jesus Christ.

For a variety of reasons, scholars today are increasingly of the view that 2 Thessalonians was written much later than 1 Thessalonians, and by a different author, whose concern was to oppose the view that 'Jesus has already come'. If 2 Thessalonians is by Paul, then it must have been written quite soon after 1 Thessalonians, when Paul and Silvanus were still together. It is difficult, however, to find a really plausible setting for the letter on the assumption of Pauline authorship.

Thanksgiving

3-12 We ought to thank God always for you, brothers and sisters, as is proper, because your faith is increasing remarkably, and the love of each one of you for the other is on the increase, so that we ourselves rest our boast on you, among the churches of God, because of your courage and faith in the midst of all your persecutions and oppressions that you put up with, [which is] evidence of God's righteous judgement, to count you worthy of the kingdom of God, for whose sake you are suffering, since in God's eyes it is appropriate to repay those who oppress you with oppression of their own, and [to repay] you who are oppressed with relief [from oppression] along with us, at the revelation of the Lord Jesus from heaven with the angels of his power in a flaming fire, who gives out punishment to those who have not come to know God, and to those who refuse to obey the gospel of our Lord Jesus, who will pay the penalty of eternal destruction, removed from the presence of the Lord and from the glory of his might, when he comes to be glorified in the midst of his saints, and to be a source of wonder for all who believe, because our witness has been shown to be reliable in you, on that day; to which end, we pray all the time about you, that our God may make you worthy of [your] call, and fulfil all [your] desire or goodness, and the work of faith in power, so that the name of our Lord Jesus may be glorified among you, and you in him, according to the grace of our God and the Lord Jesus Christ.

This difficult passage, where several words could be translated in a number of ways, is a single sentence in Greek, though the author manages it with some assurance. We can use the thanksgiving of Pauline letters as an indicator of the themes uppermost in the author's mind. Here the interest is principally on Jesus' fearsome Second Coming, and the Thessalonians' present difficulties, and the importance of them not getting despondent.

Is Jesus' Second Coming something to be feared, or something to be welcomed?

The instruction to the brethren

2 1,2 We ask you, brothers and sisters, with regard to the coming of our Lord Jesus Christ, and our being gathered to him, not to be quickly shaken from your way of thinking, neither through the Spirit, nor through the word, not through any letter supposedly from us, saying that the Day of the Lord has come.

Clearly the issue is that some people have been saying that the Day of the Lord has come (we shall see later with what undesirable consequences), and they have been claiming that Paul has lent his backing to this view.

What must come before the Day of the Lord

3, 4 Don't let anyone deceive you in any way. Because [that day will not come] unless the Rebellion comes first, and [unless] the Man of Iniquity [is revealed], the Son of Destruction, the Adversary and the One who exalts himself above everything that is called a god or an object of worship, to the point of taking his seat in the Temple of God and making himself out to be a god.

Before the end, there has to be (according to the author) a rebellion, and the revealing of the Rebellious One. Scholars have not been able to identify this character with any historical person, nor even with any celestial or infernal figure.

The reader will notice that in the second sentence above the word 'unless' makes us look for a main verb, which never appears.

Rebellion and the Lawless One

5-12 Don't you remember that when I was still with you I used to tell you these things? Now you know what is restraining him, so that he may be revealed at his own proper time. For the mystery of iniquity is already at work, only until the one who is restraining [it] is removed from the scene. And then the Lawless One will be revealed, whom the Lord Jesus will destroy with the breath of his mouth, and will annihilate him at the manifestation of his Presence. The coming of the Lawless One, by the activity of Satan with all false power, signs and portents, and all deceptive iniquity for those who are being destroyed, because they did not accept the love of truth so as to be saved. And because of this God is sending them a deceiving power, so that they should believe what is false, that all those who did not believe the truth, but consented to unrighteousness, should be condemned.

This passage is far from easy to understand, still less to translate, and scholars are not agreed on how to read it, though the basic meaning is clear: there is to be an apostasy before the end-time, and there will be a 'Lawless One' who is somehow restrained, by a 'thing' or a 'person'; and the opponents of God are going to be condemned.

Is it dangerous to start speculating about the end of the world? Are we wasting our time thinking about it at all?

Keep going; God is at work

13-17 We ought to thank God always for you, fellow Christians beloved by the Lord, because God has chosen you as first-fruits for salvation through sanctification by the Spirit and by faith in the truth, to which he has called you through our gospel, to possess the glory of our Lord Jesus Christ. So then, brothers and sisters, stand firm and hold fast to the traditions which you have been taught, whether by what we said or by what we wrote. The Lord Jesus Christ himself and God our Father who loved us and who give unfailing comfort and good hope in grace, comfort your hearts, and strengthen them in every good work and deed.

This exhortation is a little bit vague, but the readers or hearers of this letter are to keep going, confident that the Lord Jesus Christ and God our Father (note the unusual order here) are guiding the enterprise.

What is the relationship between 'the Lord Jesus Christ' and 'God our Father'?

Prayer and reassurance

3 1-5 For the rest, keep on praying for us, brothers and sisters, that the word of the Lord may run freely and be glorified, as it has done also with you, that we may be delivered from evil and wicked people. For not everybody has faith. The Lord is faithful, and he will strengthen you and guard you from the evil one. We rely on the Lord with regard to you, because you are doing, and will continue to do, what we command. May the Lord direct your hearts to the love of God and to the constancy of Christ.

This exhortation is not very specific but both the hearers and the author are to pray for each other, and they can rely on God.

Final exhortation: keep everyone hard at work

6-15 We command you, brothers and sisters, in the name of our Lord Jesus Christ, that you should try to avoid any fellow Christian who behaves in an undisciplined manner, and not in accordance with the tradition that they have received from us. For you yourselves know how you are to imitate us, because we were not undisciplined [when we were] among you, nor did we eat bread at anyone's house without payment; no – we worked, toiling and labouring night and day so as not to be a burden to any of you. This was not because we had not the right [to be fed], but so that we should offer ourselves as a model to you, for you to imitate us. For indeed when we were with you, we commanded you this, that 'if anyone is unwilling to work, let them not eat, either'.

For we hear that some of you are behaving in an undisciplined manner, not being busy at work, but on the contrary behaving like 'busybodies'. We beg and command people like this in the Lord Jesus Christ that they should work peacefully and so eat their own food. As for you, brothers and sisters, don't give up on doing what is good.

And if anyone fails to obey our teaching in this letter, take note of that person; have nothing to do with him or her, that they may be ashamed. Don't think of them as an enemy – but just admonish them as a brother or sister.

Obviously one of the purposes of the letter has been to deal with Christians who thought that the coming of the Day meant that they no longer had to work. The author is very opposed to anything that looks like 'indiscipline', and uses Paul's 'receive' and 'tradition' vocabulary to make the point. It is quite characteristic of Paul to use himself as an example for young Christians, and, under certain circumstances, to contemplate expulsion from the community of believers. 2 Thessalonians is a good document to read when we get the gloomy feeling that all was sweetness and light in the early Church, and that it has been getting worse ever since.

Does Christianity carry with it the danger that believers might feel that they don't need to work?

Closing greeting

16-18 May the Lord of peace himself grant you peace, through all and in every way.
The Lord be with all of you.

The greeting in my handwriting: PAUL, which is the identifying mark in every letter – this is how I write.

The grace of our Lord Jesus Christ be with all of you.

The closing greeting is familiar enough, down to the reference to Paul's handwriting. It is curious, however, that the 'identifying mark' seems to refer to a whole collection of letters by Paul, when, if 2 Thessalonians were really his composition, it would be only the second of his surviving letters. It still makes interesting reading, however.

The First Letter to Timothy

The First Letter to Timothy

Opening greetings

1 1,2 Paul, an apostle of Christ Jesus, by the command of God our Saviour, and Christ Jesus our Hope, to Timothy, true child in the faith, grace, mercy and peace from God our Father and Christ Jesus our Lord.

With these words we start the 'Pastoral Epistles', two addressed to Timothy and one to Titus, which come as a set, and which almost no modern scholar would ascribe to Paul's hand (though Luke Timothy Johnson's recent commentary in the Anchor Bible series makes a worthy attempt at such ascription). The first argument against Paul's authorship is that despite the occasional personal asides, the vocabulary seems different from that of Paul's undisputed letters. The second is that the Church organisation presupposed in these letters seems to reflect that of the end of the first century and the beginning of the second, rather than what you find in Paul's lifetime. In the foregoing passage, God as 'Saviour' and Christ as 'Hope' are unusual titles. And the attentive reader will note the insertion of 'mercy', a common theme in the Pastorals, between the more familiar Pauline terms 'grace and peace'.

What kind of thing do you think that Paul might say to a young church leader today?

Beware of false teaching

3-11 As I asked you to stay on at Ephesus while I journeyed into Macedonia, for you to command certain people not to teach a different doctrine and not to pay attention to stories and endless genealogies, which provide useless speculation rather than the dispensation of God in faith. But the aim of [my] command is love, whose source is a pure heart and a good conscience, and a faith that involves no pretence. Some people have gone wide of the mark of all these things, and have turned to futile talk, because they wanted to be 'teachers of the law', with no idea what they were saying, nor what they were making such confident assertions about. We know that the law is good, if someone makes use of it in a lawful way, knowing that the law is not instituted for the righteous person, but for the people who are lawless, rebellious, impious, sinners, unholy and godless, who kill their mother and father, murderers, fornicators, sodomites, kidnappers, liars and perjurers, and anything else that contradicts healthy teaching, according to the glorious gospel of blessed God, with which I myself have been entrusted.

It is virtually impossible to reconstruct the enemies that the author has in mind; and indeed it is hard to imagine this entire list of vices contained within a single person or even school of thought; but the author is warning of the kind of thing that is likely to go on once you start to 'teach a different doctrine'.

The leaving of Timothy in Ephesus while Paul went to Macedonia does not fit anything that we know of from Paul's correspondence or from Acts; but that need not matter; if Paul did not write this letter, then these details would be the author's attempt to give the letter a Pauline 'feel', when its function is to answer the question, 'What would Paul be saying to us today?' One of the tendencies that we shall see in the Pastorals is a desire to keep doctrine under control, because of the undesirable consequences of getting it wrong.

What 'useless speculation' might Paul warn against today?

Paul's own experience of God's mercy

12-17 I give thanks to Christ Jesus our Lord, who empowered me, because he thought me trustworthy enough to appoint me for ministry; I had earlier been a blasphemer and a persecutor and braggart; but I was treated with mercy, because what I did as an unbeliever [was done through] ignorance; but the grace of our Lord was present in great abundance, with faith and love in Jesus Christ. The saying is reliable, and worthy of approval, that 'Christ Jesus came into the world to save sinners', of which I am number one. But for this reason I was treated with mercy, that in me first of all Christ Jesus might show all his forbearance, as a prototype of those who would believe in him to [receive] eternal life. To the king of the ages, the immortal, invisible, only God, [be] honour and glory for ever and ever. Amen.

The contrast here between human sinfulness and God's mercy is there in the undisputed letters of Paul; but it is worth noticing the tendency here to rationalise Paul's previous persecution of the Church, that he 'didn't know what he was doing'.

The expression 'the saying is reliable' appears five times in the Pastorals (1 Timothy 1:15; 3:1; 4:9; 2 Timothy 2:11; Titus 3:8), and not at all in the certainly genuine letters of Paul.

What has Christ Jesus done for Paul?

A command to Timothy

18-20 This command I entrust to you, Timothy, my child, in accordance with the former prophecies about you, that in them you may fight the good fight, with faith and a good conscience, which some people have rejected with regard to the faith, and been shipwrecked. Examples of this are Hymenaeus and Alexander, whom I have handed over to Satan, that they may learn not to blaspheme.

It is quite hard to know precisely what is the command that the author is enjoining on Timothy, unless it refers to all that follows. When, on the other hand, it seems that we are coming to a concrete case, that of Hymenaeus and Alexander, we have no evidence whatever as to what the problem was.

Prayers for everybody

2 1-7 First of all, I ask that petitions and prayers and intercessions and acts of thanksgiving be made on behalf of all people, on behalf of kings and all those who are in authority, so that we may live a tranquil and quiet life, in all piety and

holiness. This is good and acceptable before our Saviour God, who wants everybody to be saved and come to the recognition of the truth. For,

'there is one God
and one mediator between God and humanity,
the human being Jesus Christ
who gave himself as a ransom for all,
a testimony at the proper time.'

For this I was appointed a herald and an apostle (I am speaking the truth; I am not lying), a teacher of the Gentiles in faith and truth.

Some of this sounds very much like the real Paul, such as the reference to his mission, and the remark that 'I am speaking the truth; I am not lying' – see Romans 9:1; 2 Corinthians 11:31; Galatians 1:20). But the attentive reader will notice the reference once again to the 'Saviour God' and the understanding of salvation as coming 'to the recognition of the truth', which is not how the Paul who wrote Galatians, Romans and 1 Corinthians would have expressed it.

What is the author's understanding of Jesus Christ?

The conduct of women

2 8–3 1a So I want the men to pray in every place, lifting up holy hands without any anger or argument. In just the same way, [I want] women to adorn themselves with tasteful deportment, in modesty and restraint, not with braided hair or gold or pearls or expensive clothing, but in a manner that is fitting for women who lay claim to reverence for God, through good works. Let a wife do her learning in tranquillity, in all submission. However I do not permit a wife to do any teaching, nor to have authority over a husband – she must be in tranquillity. For Adam was formed first, then Eve. And it was not Adam who was deceived; it was his wife who was deceived and fell into transgression. But she will be saved by childbearing, provided that they remain in faith and love and holiness, along with self-control. The saying is reliable.

Nowadays we read this passage with some embarrassment, and want to reassert the basic Christian (and Pauline) insight that all people, including both men and women, are equal before God; but here women are told how they may dress, and what their role is in the Christian Church, namely to be quiet, and not to have authority. This claim, which will not be congenial to many readers today, is then supported by an argument from Scripture, slightly reminiscent of Paul's argument in 1 Corinthians 11, but not really attentive to the actual text of Genesis. It is important to see this passage in context. Our author is of a conservative cast of mind, writing at a time when, all over the Mediterranean world, women were adopting a higher profile, and at this stage of the Church's development he does not wish to give the enemies of Christianity grounds for criticism. It does not mean that today Christian women must be 'silent and submissive'.

Do you think that there should be a difference between the roles played by men and women in the Church?

The qualities of an 'overseer': don't rock the boat

1b-7 If anyone aspires to the office of 'overseer', it is a good job that he desires. So the 'overseer' must be irreproachable, the husband of [only] one woman, temperate, self-controlled, respectable, hospitable, a good teacher, not addicted to wine nor a bully. No – he should be gentle, peaceable, not obsessed with money, well able to take care of his own household, keeping his children in good order, with complete dignity (if he has no idea how to conduct his own household, how is he going to take care of the Church of God?). He should not be a recent convert, so that he doesn't get conceited, and fall under the devil's condemnation. He must also have a good reputation among non-Christians, so that he doesn't fall into disgrace, which is a devil's snare.

The Greek word for 'overseer' turned eventually into the English word 'bishop', but at this stage it is not at all clear what the function was, so it is better in translation to use a word that reflects the basic meaning. We notice that the overseer is to be a family man, and to have no publicly obvious moral flaws. Those who argue against Paul's authorship of this letter point out that the two conditions at the end, about the overseer not being a recent convert, and having a good reputation among non-Christians, would, so the argument goes, be unimaginable in Paul's day; almost everyone would have been a 'neophyte' (new convert), so this could not have been a disqualification for Church leadership in Corinth. Similarly, Paul expected the Church to be persecuted by outsiders, so he would never have made public esteem from non-Christians a qualification for holding office within the Church. The author is writing in an age where Christianity needed acceptance from outsiders.

To what extent should these criteria be operative for Church leaders today? Why should they have a good reputation among non-Christians?

The qualities of a 'servant'

8-13 'Servants' likewise should be honourable, not insincere, nor addicted to lots of wine, nor greedy for dishonest gain; they should hold the mystery of faith with a clean conscience. And these people should be tested first; then let them serve, if they are irreproachable.

Their wives should likewise be honourable, not slanderers, but temperate, faithful in every respect. 'Servants' should be husbands of only one wife, well able to take care of their children, and of their own households. For those who perform their service becomingly win a good standing for themselves, and much assurance in the [life of] faith in Christ Jesus.

The word translated as 'servants' is that which eventually turned into the English word 'deacon'. It is noticeable that 'servants' or 'deacons' require very much the same qualities as 'overseers' or 'bishops' in the preceding verses; presumably the author and his readers know the difference.

A sentence in the middle might either refer to women 'deacons' or to the wives of such 'servants' – it is impossible to be sure.

Why is it important for the wives of Church officials to be of a certain character?

Christ in the Church

14-16 I am writing this, hopeful of coming to you soon. But if I delay, I want you to
know how one must behave in the house of God, which is the Church of the Living
God, the pillar and foundation of the truth. And, undeniably, the mystery of godliness
is a great one, who

'appeared in the flesh,
was justified in the Spirit,
appeared to angels,
was proclaimed among the Gentiles,
was believed in the world,
was taken up in glory.'

This rather odd passage starts with a colourable account of how the letter might fit into the life of Paul, but continues the emphasis on behaviour in the Church (which at this stage, of course, is a community not a building), and relates it to the presence of Christ, the 'mystery of godliness'. What the author says here lacks the warmth with which Paul ordinarily speaks of his beloved Jesus.

Warning against opponents

4 1-5 The Spirit explicitly says that at the last times some people will fall away from
the faith, paying attention to deceptive spirits and the teachings of demons,
with the hypocrisy of liars, branded in their own consciences, discouraging marriage,
[telling people] to abstain from foods which God had created for the faithful and
those who know the truth to accept gratefully. Because everything created by God is
good; it is not to be rejected but to be accepted gratefully. For it is made holy by
God's word and by prayer.

If we can filter out the propaganda here, the author is warning against those who are over-keen on asceticism, especially those who advocate celibacy and selective approaches to food (such as vegetarianism, for example). 'We are not fanatics' would appear to be his slogan for dealing with the outside world.

What is the difference between taking one's religion seriously and being a fanatic?

Timothy's task

6-10 If you make this known to the brothers and sisters, you will be a good servant of
Christ Jesus, nourished by the words of the faith and of the correct teaching which
you have followed; but reject the profane stories of old women. Train yourself for
godliness; for physical training is of little use, whereas godliness is useful for every-
thing, since it holds the promise of life now ***and*** life to come. The saying is reliable
and worthy to be accepted by all. For that is the point of our labour and struggle, that

our hope is in the Living God, who is Saviour of all people, especially of those who do believe.

This tells Timothy, in the most general terms, what he is to do. Timothy is described here as a 'servant' or 'deacon', which may suggest that the word has not yet taken on a precise hierarchical sense. The reader will notice that the final sentence is grist to the mill of those who cannot believe in a God who condemns all unbelievers, simply because of being unbelievers; for this author, God is the Saviour of all people.

We notice a third example of the expression, the 'saying is reliable'.

Is the Living God the Saviour of all people, or only of those who believe?

Timothy the teacher

11-16 Insist on these things, and teach them. Let no one show contempt for your youthfulness; instead, become a model for believers, in word, in behaviour, in love, in faith, in all propriety. While I am coming, pay attention to reading, and exhortation, and teaching. Never neglect the gift of grace which was given you through prophecy, along with the laying-on of hands of the council of elders. Put these things into practice; be [immersed] in them, that your progress may be evident to all. Be attentive to yourself and to your teaching; remain steadfast in them. For if you do this, you will save both yourself and those who hear you.

This is how the Christian teacher is to operate; if the letter is not by Paul, the instruction has been given a veil of personal detail to cover the fiction. Regardless of whether or not Paul wrote it, however, it could still be an instruction to teachers today.

What do you think was the 'gift of grace' given to Timothy 'through prophecy, along with the laying-on of hands'?

Domestic relations in the Church

5 1-22 Don't strike an older man; instead, encourage him as your father. Treat younger men like your brothers, older women like your mother, younger women as your sisters – in all purity.

Widows: honour those who are genuinely widows; but if a widow has children or grandchildren, let them first learn to act piously towards their own household, and to make a return to their forebears. For this is pleasing to God. The genuine widow, however, who has been left on her own, has placed her hope in God, and sticks at her intercessions and prayers night and day – but the one who lives a life of self-indulgence is already dead. Give them this command, that they should be irreproachable; but if someone does not take care of their own people, and particularly of their own family, they have denied the faith and are worse than an unbeliever.

A person should not be registered as a widow under the age of sixty, and [only] married once; she should have a reputation for good works; it is conditional upon her having brought up children, having given hospitality to strangers, having washed the feet of the saints, having come to the aid of those in trouble, and devoted herself to every good work. Don't accept younger widows; for whenever sensuality turns them against Christ, they want to get married, and they come under condemnation because of abandoning their first commitment. At the same time they are lazy, and they go round [people's] houses; and it's not just that they are lazy – but they are also gossips and busybodies, and they talk about things that they should not.

So I want ***younger women*** to get married, to have children, to manage their household, to give the adversary no pretext for abuse. For already some have turned aside to follow Satan. If some woman believer has widows [in her family] she should look after them, and not let the Church be burdened, so that the Church may look after the real widows.

Elders who show themselves good leaders are to be accounted worthy of double salary, especially those who work at preaching and teaching. For Scripture says, 'You shall not muzzle the threshing ox' and 'The worker is worthy of his hire'. Don't accept an accusation against an elder, unless it is 'on the word of two or three witnesses'. Reprimand those who sin publicly, so that the others may show wariness. I solemnly charge you, by God and Christ Jesus and the chosen angels, that you observe these things without prejudice, doing nothing in a spirit of partiality. Don't be in a hurry to lay hands on [or: 'ordain'] anyone, and don't take part in other people's sins. Keep yourself pure.

The regulations dealing with how various sectors in the Church should treat each other, and the criteria for being enrolled as a widow, are now almost beyond our reach. For example, Timothy has to be warned not to hit an older man (but presumably **could** *strike a younger man!), and 'not to be in a hurry to lay hands on anyone' (but presumably might if he does it after a pause for reflection), whereas we live in an age that is less at ease with corporal punishment. The author's animadversions on 'merry widows', and his sense that they should 'marry, have children, and run the household' do not today find a ready reception, even though they could be read as stressing the importance of the woman's role in Church and society.*

The word for 'elder' has turned into the English word 'priest'; and the instruction about not accepting accusations against them, except where there are two or three witnesses, has posed problems in our day.

All that having been said, a society where everyone knows their part and plays it, not out of compulsion, but enthusiastically, because that is what they want to do, can be a happier place than many that we see today.

How many of these rules for Church personnel would be helpful today?

Some instructions, with no particular theme

5[23–]6[2a] Stop drinking water, but make use of a little wine, for your stomach's sake, and your frequent attacks of weakness.

Some people's sins are known to all, going ahead of them to judgement; while others they follow. In just the same way, good deeds are known to all, and those that are otherwise cannot be indefinitely suppressed.

Those who are slaves under the yoke, let them regard their own masters as worthy of all honour, so that God's name and teaching should not be blasphemed. But those who have masters who are believers should not despise them because they are fellow Christians; but they should be all the more enslaved to them because they are believers and beloved, those who devote themselves to good service.

The material seems less well organised at this point, a pseudo-medical injunction, which probably does not contradict the criterion for 'overseers' that we saw in 3:3 – that had to do with **addiction** *to wine! Then comes a general comment about people's deeds becoming known (whether it refers to elders or to the congregation as a whole is not clear). Finally, there are instructions to slaves who are, frankly, told not to get above themselves if they belong to a Christian master. Again, we no longer belong in a world where the institution of slavery can go unquestioned, and we struggle to think our way into such a world. Our author is undoubtedly somewhat conservative in his social attitudes – but he is also well aware of the need to make Christianity acceptable to his contemporaries.*

What is the Christian attitude to slavery? Has it always been so?

A collection of teachings

2b-19 Teach and exhort these things. If someone teaches a different doctrine, and if they do not agree with the health-giving words of our Lord Jesus Christ, and the teaching that goes along with godliness, they are conceited, knowing nothing. They have a sick craving for controversies and verbal squabbles, from which come envy, strife, blasphemies, wicked suspicions, and the mutual friction of people whose morals are corrupted and deprived of the truth, because they suppose that godliness is a way to make money.

Now [it is true] that godliness, with self-sufficiency, is enormously profitable, for

'we brought nothing into the world,
because neither can we take anything out of it.
If we have food and covering,
we shall be satisfied with these'.

But those who wish to be wealthy fall into the tempting trap of many senseless and harmful desires, which plunge people into death and destruction. For the root of all evils is the love of money. Some people have lusted for money and wandered away from the truth, and have been shot through with many pains.

But you, O man of God, flee from these things.
Look for righteousness, godliness, faith,
love, fortitude, gentleness.
Play the great game of faith;
take hold of the everlasting life to which you have been called,
and make the great acknowledgement before many witnesses.

I charge you, before the God who gives life to all things, and before Christ Jesus, who bore testimony under Pontius Pilate to the great acknowledgement, to keep the commandment spotless and without reproach until the appearance of our Lord Jesus Christ, which

he will show at his own proper time [– he who is]
the blessed and sole Sovereign
the King of all who reign as kings
the Lord of all who rule as lords,
the One who alone has immortality,
dwelling in unapproachable light,
which no human has seen or is able to see,
to whom be honour and eternal power. Amen.

Impress upon the wealthy in the present age not to think haughty thoughts, nor to set their hopes on the uncertainty of riches. Instead, [they should have their hopes set on] God, who provides us with everything richly for our enjoyment; they should be doing good, rich in good deeds, generous, ready to share, laying up for themselves a good foundation for the future, that they may take hold of what is ***really*** life.

One major problem that the author sees is that of wealth, and in this respect, 1 Timothy may have much to say to a consumerist and materialist society that appears to have lost its way.

The 'great acknowledgement' mentioned above is something that Timothy has to do, both as Church leader and as Christian; it is also something that Jesus has already done. What precisely the author has in mind is not absolutely clear, but it is at least 'standing up to be counted' and telling the truth, no matter how risky.

Are we called to make this 'acknowledgement' or 'confession'?

Concluding greetings

20, 21 O Timothy, keep what has been entrusted; turn aside from profane and empty talk and the contradictions of what is falsely called knowledge, which some people have professed, and have gone wide of the mark of faith.

Grace be with you.

This is not quite the conclusion that we should expect from what we know of other Pauline letters; there are, for example, no greetings to or from anyone but Timothy. On the other hand, this letter is only written to Timothy. If we knew more about the situation that the author has in mind, we should be able to comment more exactly on what he is really saying.

The author speaks of 'the contradictions of what is falsely called knowledge': what would be the equivalent today?

The Second Letter to Timothy

The Second Letter to Timothy

This differs in many ways from 1 Timothy, though some of the issues remain the same. It is much more personal, and far more names are mentioned. It can also be described as Paul's 'last will and testament', and for some scholars this is the most likely of the three 'Pastoral Letters' actually to have come from Paul's hand. It has far more echoes of other Pauline letters than we find in 1 Timothy or Titus.

Opening greetings

1 1,2 Paul, an apostle of Christ Jesus through the will of God, with a view to the promise of life which is in Christ Jesus, to [my] beloved child Timothy, grace, mercy and peace from God the Father and Christ Jesus our Lord.

As in the opening of 1 Timothy, the author has inserted 'mercy' between the standard Pauline pair of 'grace' and 'peace'. Otherwise this is a characteristic Pauline introduction.

Thanksgiving and overture

3-14 I give thanks to God, whom I worship, following my ancestors, with a clear conscience, when I make unceasing remembrance of you in my prayers, night and day, [because] I long to see you, in order to be filled with joy when I receive a reminder of your unfeigned faith, which dwelt first in your grandmother Lois and your mother Eunice, and (I am persuaded) also in you. For this reason I am reminding you to rekindle God's gift of grace, which is in you through the laying-on of my hands. For God did not give us a spirit of cowardice, but a spirit of power and love and of self-discipline. Don't, therefore, be ashamed of witnessing to our Lord, nor of me, his prisoner. Instead, join [with me/us] in suffering for the gospel, under the power of God,

who saved us
and called us with a holy calling
not because of our works
but because of his own purpose and grace
which was given us in Christ Jesus
before the eternal ages and has now appeared
through the appearance of our Saviour Christ Jesus,
who has destroyed death
and brought life and immortality to light through the gospel

for which I was appointed herald, apostle and teacher. That is also the reason that I am suffering these things. But I'm not embarrassed, because I know in whom I have put my trust; and I am persuaded that he has the power to preserve my deposit for that day. You have a model of healthy words which you heard from me in the faith and the love [that is] in Christ Jesus. Keep the noble trust through the Holy Spirit who dwells in us.

The thanksgiving is always a part of a Pauline letter, but (in keeping with the rest of this letter) this one is very personal, with its reference to Lois and Eunice. If Paul is writing shortly before his execution in the mid-60s AD, then that is just about enough time for Timothy to be a third-generation Christian. As in 1 Timothy, there is a relative clause introducing a reference to the 'Saviour', and to Paul's 'appointment' (as 'herald, apostle and teacher'; see 1 Timothy 1:1; 2:7).

Why might Timothy be ashamed of 'witnessing to our Lord' or of Paul?

Personal details: traitors and helpers

15-18 You know that all those in Asia turned their backs on me, among whom were Phygelos and Hermogenes; may the Lord grant mercy to the house of Onesiphorus, because he frequently refreshed me, and was not embarrassed by my imprisonment; but when he got to Rome he promptly sought me out and found me. May the Lord grant him to find mercy from the Lord on that day; and you know better [than I do] what great services he rendered in Ephesus.

We know nothing about any of these names; but they have a ring about them, and it is hard to see why a forger would have included them.

Advice to a young minister

2 1-7 But you, my child, be empowered by the grace that is in Christ Jesus, and the things that you have heard from me before many witnesses, entrust them to reliable people, who will be competent to teach others. Take your share of suffering hardship, like a good soldier of Christ Jesus. No one who is on active service gets entangled in civilian pursuits, in order to satisfy the one who recruited him. But if someone competes in a race, they don't get the gold medal unless they have competed in accordance with the rules. The labouring farmer should be the first to have a share in the crop. Think what I am saying; for the Lord will give you insight in every respect.

Timothy might, after all, be very young indeed, perhaps a teenager, who is finding his vocation difficult, and not easily able to grasp Paul's teaching. Here Paul offers three metaphors, from soldiering, sports and farming, each with a slightly different point: Timothy should focus on what he is doing, operate according to the rules, and then expect to get his reward.

Have you ever had to suffer 'hardship, like a good soldier of Christ Jesus'?

The message: Christ is all

8-13 Remember Jesus Christ who was raised from the dead, of the seed of David, according to my gospel because of which I am suffering evil, even imprisonment like a criminal – but God's word can't be locked up. Therefore I endure everything on account of the elect, that they too may gain salvation that is in Christ Jesus, along with eternal glory. The saying is sure:

For if we have died with him, we shall also live with him.
If we endure, we shall also reign with him.
If we disown [him], he will also disown us.
If we are faithless, he remains faithful.
For he cannot disown himself.

This is a kind of summary of the author's message. Timothy must concentrate on Christ and, as always with Paul, above all on Christ's death and Resurrection, and the need for Christians to belong to that mystery and not to try to evade its uncomfortable consequences.

Do Christians find it easy to forget Jesus?

Coping with false teachers

14-26 Remember these things as you adjure [people] before God not to go in for verbal quibbles, which serve no useful purpose, [but only] to destroy those who hear them. Be eager to present yourself to God as tried and tested, a worker with nothing to be ashamed of, who cuts a straight path for the word of truth. But avoid godless and empty chatterings, for they will make ever-greater advances in impiety, and their word will devour like cancer [or: eat its way like gangrene]. Among these are Hymenaeus and Philetus, who have gone astray with regard to the truth, claiming that the Resurrection has already taken place; and they are overturning some people's faith. But God's solid foundation stands firm, and it has this seal, 'The Lord knows those who are his' and 'Let them keep away from wickedness, all those who name the Lord's name'. In a great house, there are not only gold and silver vessels; there are also vessels of wood and of earthenware; and some are for honourable use, others for dishonourable use. So if people cleanse themselves from these things, they will be a vessel for honourable use, sanctified, useful to the master, prepared for every [kind of] good work.

Avoid youthful desires; make a thing of righteousness, faith, love, peace, along with those who call upon the Lord out of a pure heart. Discourage stupid and uneducated speculations; be aware that they breed quarrels. But the Lord's slaves must not quarrel; they should be gentle to all, good at teaching, forbearing, gently correcting opponents. It might perhaps be the case that God will give them a change of heart, leading to knowledge of the truth, and they may come to their senses and escape the devil's trap, those who have been held captive by him to perform his will.

More than anything else, the author is concerned to discourage false teaching; he is painfully aware of the damage it can do, and uses an alarming medical metaphor for it: cancer (or perhaps 'gangrene'). He uses three other metaphors here, that of a forester, who 'cuts a straight path', that of earthenware vessels, also used in 2 Corinthians 4:7 (and see also Romans 9:21), and (an old Pauline favourite), that of a building or 'great house' for the Church (see especially 1 Corinthians 3:9-17). All three images point to the function of a Church leader to ensure that orthodoxy is preserved.

The challenge for our day may be to accept this challenge, while avoiding the dead hand and repellent tedium that the word 'orthodoxy' can sometimes project.

For a positive understanding of orthodoxy, however, the reader is recommended to read G. K. Chesterton's book of that title, which has still much to say to us today.

Do you find 'orthodoxy' a repellent or tedious idea?

Problems at the end-time

3 1-9 Know this, that in the last days difficult times will be threatening. For people will appear who are lovers of self and lovers of money, braggarts and arrogant blasphemers who disobey their parents, ungrateful and unholy, unloving and implacable, slanderers and dissolute, untamed, unloving-of-the-good, traitors and reckless, conceited and loving pleasure rather than God, people who have the appearance of piety, but have refused its reality. These too you should avoid. For from them come those who worm their way into households and captivate silly women who are overwhelmed by their sins, who are led by desires of various kinds, who are always attending lessons, but never able to come to a knowledge of the truth. Just as Jannes and Jambres defied Moses, so these men defy the truth; they are people depraved in mind and unqualified with regard to the faith. But they will not advance any further; for their mindlessness will be evident to all, just like that of [Jannes and Jambres].

It is hard to be sure of the precise problems that the author has in mind here, but they have three aspects: moral failings, resistance to orthodoxy, and an attraction to the women members of the Church, perhaps especially those who want to study their faith in greater depth. Our author would not be the first man, nor the last, to deprecate the study of theology by women; but his problems and ours are not necessarily identical, and for us today what is of interest is the general principle rather than its particular applications.

Is it only in 'the last days' that such people appear?

On surviving the difficulties as Paul did

10-17 You, however, have carefully followed my teaching, my way of life, the tendency of my thought, my faith, patience, love, endurance, and the persecutions and sufferings that came my way in Antioch, Iconium and Lystra. I endured these persecutions, and from them the Lord delivered me. All those who want to live a godly life in Christ Jesus will be persecuted. Wicked people and charlatans will go from bad to worse, deluding and deluded. You must stick with what you have learnt and been convinced of, knowing the people from whom you learnt it. Because since you were a child you have known the sacred scriptures, which have the ability to make you wise on the way to salvation through faith in Christ Jesus. All Scripture is breathed-by-God, and useful for teaching, for refutation, for improvement, for training, that the man of God may be proficient, prepared for every good work.

If it were Paul who is writing, facing the fact of his imminent death, then it would hardly be surprising if he gave Timothy a tip or two about coping with the difficulties that lie ahead. Nor would it astonish us if he were to point to his own example as something to follow (compare 1 Corinthians 4:16; 11:1; Philippians 3:17; 1 Thessalonians 1:6).

The author's emphasis on the importance of Scripture is also quite characteristic of Paul, of course; and it would be quite normal for him to offer the Old Testament to Timothy as a way out of any difficulties.

The phrase 'every good work' can sound a bit jarring to those who think that Paul has no place for 'works' in his map of salvation, but see 2 Corinthians 9:8, and, in the Pastorals, see 1 Timothy 6:18; 2 Timothy 2:21; Titus 1:16; 3:1. Though everything is God's gift, Paul is well aware that we have to respond, by 'presenting our bodies to God as instruments of righteousness' or (in a frequent metaphor), 'running the race' (see Philippians 3:12-14; 1 Corinthians 9:24-27).

How do you interpret the words 'all Scripture is breathed-by-God'?

Urgent instructions to Timothy from the dying Paul

4 1-8 I adjure you, before God and before Christ Jesus, who is going to come to judge the living and the dead, and by his manifestation and by his kingdom: proclaim the word; be ready, whether it is convenient or inconvenient; admonish, rebuke, console, in all patience and teaching. For a time will come when they will not put up with healthy teaching; instead, they will pile up teachers for themselves, titillating their ears, and turning their ears away from the truth, while directing them towards fables. But you must stay sober in every respect, bear hardship patiently, do the job of an evangelist, fulfil your service.

As for me, I am being offered up, and the time for my death has come. I have played the great game; I have completed the race; I have kept the faith. For the future, the gold medal of righteousness is reserved for me, which the Lord, the Righteous Judge, will award me on that day; and not just me, but all those who have loved his appearing.

This is a stirring passage; it has an urgency about it, and an eye for what really matters. The author knows that death is almost upon him, and the tone of these lines makes a literary fiction hard to imagine; he wants his addressee to be clear about the task that lies before him, as Timothy picks up the baton that Paul is passing to him.

Not for the first time, he uses a metaphor from athletics, to indicate that he is almost there, and to affirm his confidence in God and in Christ (who is clearly the 'Lord' who is mentioned in the final lines). The word for 'death' is a nautical metaphor, and it refers to the activity of untying the ropes and casting off.

The notion of 'healthy' teaching is a frequent one in the Pastorals: see 1 Timothy 1:10; 6:3; 2 Timothy 1:13; Titus 1:9; 2:1, 2.

Is the author right in foreseeing a time 'when they will not put up with healthy teaching'?

The author's personal situation

9-15 Make an effort to come quickly to me. For Demas has abandoned me; he loved the present world and went off to Thessalonica, Crescens to Galatia, Titus to Dalmatia. Luke is the only one with me. Pick up Mark and bring him with you, for he is useful to me for the ministry. Tychicus I have sent to Ephesus. When you come, bring the cloak which I left in Troas, at Carpus's house, and the scrolls, especially the parchments. Alexander the coppersmith did me great harm. The Lord will repay him according to his deeds. Watch out for him – for he is utterly opposed to our teaching.

There are several names here; none of them can be identified with any certainty. Though some of the names appear in other Pauline letters and in Acts, we do not know if they refer to the same people. So we cannot say whether the 'Luke' and 'Mark' mentioned here have anything to do with the gospels that bear those names. The reader gains a sense of a Church on the move, which certainly squares with both Acts and the indisputably genuine Paulines.

What sense do you get here of the life of early Christian missionaries?

The apostle is never utterly abandoned

16-18 In my first defence, no one was at my side; they ***all*** abandoned me. May it not be put down to their account. But the Lord stood by me and empowered me, that the preaching might be fulfilled through me, and that all the Gentiles might hear; and I was delivered from the lion's mouth. The Lord will deliver me from every evil deed, and will save me for his heavenly kingdom. To him be the glory for ever and ever. Amen.

We cannot say what this 'first defence' might have been; but the author's faith comes powerfully through the text. There is nothing that can finally dismay him – or us.

'The Lord stood by me': have you ever experienced this in difficult or dangerous circumstances?

Final salutations

19-22 Greet Prisca and Aquila, and the house of Onesiphorus. Erastus stayed in Corinth, and I left Trophimus at Miletus – he was sick. Make an effort to come before winter. Greetings to you from Euboulos and Pudens and Linus and Claudia, and all the brothers and sisters.

The Lord be with your spirit. Grace be with you.

We know some of these names, notably Prisca and Aquila, and Erastus, but not others (except that Onesiphorus appears at 1:16). There is a profound longing for Timothy to come soon; on the whole, winter was not propitious for travelling around the Mediterranean basin: storms at sea and snow on the mountains made marine and land journeys equally problematic.

The Letter to Titus

The Letter to Titus

Like 1 and 2 Timothy, Titus is regarded by most scholars as not being by Paul (although see Luke Timothy Johnson's commentary in the Anchor Bible series for a vigorous presentation of the case for Pauline authorship).

Opening greetings

1 1-4 Paul, a slave of God, and an apostle of Jesus Christ, according to the faith of God's elect, and according to the knowledge of the truth in accordance with godliness, in the hope of eternal life, which God, who is free of all deceit, promised before the eternal ages, and has revealed his word in his own proper time by the preaching with which I was entrusted by the command of our Saviour God, to Titus, true child according to the common faith, grace and peace from God the Father and Christ Jesus our Saviour.

This is a single sentence, longer and more complex than the opening greetings in the other Pastoral Letters. The word 'Saviour' is used twice in this passage, once of God and the second time of Christ Jesus. 'Faith' is a matter of content rather than commitment. It also emphasises Paul's own commission, introduced, as elsewhere in the two letters to Timothy, by a relative clause.

The job of an 'overseer', in Crete and elsewhere

5-9 This was the reason that I left you in Crete, for you to put right what remains, and set up elders in individual cities, as I myself commanded you, provided someone is irreproachable, the husband of only one wife, who has children who are of the faith, are not accused of debauchery, or rebellious. For the 'overseer' must be irreproachable as God's steward, not self-willed, not quick-tempered, nor addicted to wine, not a bully, nor fond of dishonest gain, but hospitable, loving all that is good, temperate, righteous, holy, self-controlled, holding fast to the teaching of the trustworthy message, that he may be able also to comfort with sound teaching and refute opponents.

We notice here that 'overseer' and 'elder' are used as equivalent; and the office described here demands more or less the same qualities as the officials mentioned in 1 Timothy 3. Modern Church leaders may be alarmed at the requirement that their children should be believers, and not profligate or rebellious.

'Comfort with sound teaching and refute opponents': is this the function of a Church official today?

The opponents in Crete

10-16 For there are many who are rebellious, who go in for meaningless discussions, and create illusions – especially those of the Circumcision Party. These people must be silenced – they turn entire households upside down by teaching what they should not, in order to make a base profit. One of them, one of their very own prophets, said,

'Cretans are always liars, vicious brutes, idle gluttons.'

The testimony is true. For that reason, reprimand them severely, that they may be healthy in the faith, not paying any attention to Jewish fables and the commands of human beings who repudiate the truth. Everything is clean for those who are clean; but for those who are tainted and unbelievers, nothing is clean – their understanding and their consciences are tainted. They claim to know God, but deny it by what they do; they are detestable and intractable, and incapable of any good work.

Here it looks as though the opponents that the author has in mind are Jewish Christians, wanting to observe the dietary laws of the Old Testament. Apart from the references to Cretans, these animadversions could apply to anyone who Paul thought was going back on the freedom of the gospel. It is worth noticing, perhaps, that there is not a single church built in the name of St Paul in the whole island of Crete.

'These people must be silenced': is there wisdom as well as an obvious danger in this notion?

Household code

2 1-10 As for you, say the things that are appropriate for healthy teaching.

- Tell the ***older men*** to be sober, dignified, healthy in faith, love and perseverance.
- Tell the ***older women***, likewise, to be sober in their behaviour, not slanderers, nor addicted to lots of wine; they are to teach what is noble and good,
- so that they may encourage the ***young women*** to love their husbands; they should love their children, be temperate, pure, good household managers, and submissive to their own husbands – so that people don't blaspheme God's word.
- Encourage the ***young men*** likewise to be temperate in every respect; offer yourself as a model of good works, and integrity in doctrine, reverence, and a sound preaching that is beyond reproach, so that the opponent may be put to shame, having nothing dreadful to say of us.
- Tell ***slaves*** to be submissive to their own masters in every respect, to be obliging rather than argumentative, not misappropriating [property], but showing all good faith, so that they make the teaching of our Saviour God attractive in every way.

As in other New Testament documents, we have here a household code, perhaps rather starker than the one in Ephesians, which was subversively suffused with love. This one, perhaps reflecting a situation wherein it seemed important to underplay the radical challenge of Christianity, seems much more inclined to go along with the status quo; slaves, for example, are told to submit to their 'masters'; the word 'Lord', which tends in other household codes to undermine the master-slave relationship, is, perhaps significantly, not used here. The passage about the 'young women' (if that is to whom it refers; grammatically, it could be a reversion to the older women) may give the clue, 'so that people don't blaspheme God's word'. Throughout its history, Christianity has had to walk uneasily between fidelity to its entirely radical message and making itself attractive to a majority that is at ease with something a little more comfortable.

Like Paul, Titus is to be fairly up-front about offering himself as an example. (The syntax of the relevant sentence is puzzling, but the meaning is clear.)

How should Christians strike the balance between being accommodating to the society we live in and being faithful to the radical demands of the gospel?

A people for Christ

11-15 For the saving grace of God has appeared to all people, correcting us, so that with moderation we may renounce ungodliness and worldly desires, and live soberly, justly and reverently in the present age, waiting for the blessed hope [which is] the appearance of the glory of our great God and Saviour Jesus Christ, who gave himself for us, in order to ransom us from [the slavery of] all iniquity, and purify for himself a chosen people, fanatical about good works. Say these things, urge them, and make the reprimands with all authority.

Let no one despise you.

There is a coherence between doctrine and ethics; if the Church is to be a place where Christ can appear, then Church leaders need to have a hand on the rudder, to make sure that the appropriate patterns of behaviour are operative, and that there are no signs of 'ungodliness' and 'worldly behaviour', and every indication of being a 'chosen people, keen on good works'. But notice that this is not a reversion to 'justification by works'; it is simply a response to the fact that 'Jesus gave himself for us in order to ransom us'.

The phrase 'the glory of our great God and Saviour Jesus Christ' is a slightly more natural reading than the alternative, which would translate 'the glory of the great God and of our Saviour Jesus Christ'. But to call Jesus 'God' is not an impossibly enormous step forward from Paul's own Christology.

Relations with authority

3 1, 2 Remind them to be submissive to rulers and authorities, to be obedient, ready for every good work, to slander nobody, to be peaceable, considerate, showing gentleness to all human beings.

Once again, we see the author's concern for the infant Church (in Crete) not to wear so radical a hat that it alienates the authorities or public opinion. There are some situations in which it is a Christian's duty to challenge fearlessly. In other circumstances it may be more appropriate to keep one's head down.

Which of these two situations do we live in today?

Why treat outsiders decently?

3-11 For we also were once foolish, disobedient, deluded, enslaved to different kinds of desires and passions, spending our lives in malice and spite, hateful and loathing one another,

'but when the kindness and love of humankind of our Saviour God made its appearance,
not in consequence of works of righteousness which we have done,
but in accordance with his mercy,
he saved us through the washing of rebirth
and the renewal of the Holy Spirit
which he poured richly upon us,
through Jesus Christ our Saviour,
so that having been made righteous by his grace,
we might become heirs in accordance with [our] hope of eternal life.

The saying is reliable; and with regard to this, I want to insist with you, that those who have come to faith in God should take care to be outstanding in good works; for these are good and beneficial to human beings. But avoid foolish speculations and genealogies and controversies and wrangles about the law. For they are useless and lead nowhere. Drive out a person who is causing divisions, after a first and a second warning; know that such a person is perverted, and sins because he is self-condemned.

This passage, couched in entirely Pauline terms, explains the previous one, on having good relations with the authorities and other non-Christians. The argument is that Christians have no cause to look down on their non-Christian neighbours, because they were in the same boat until God intervened in Christ, through no merit of theirs. This puts the onus on Christians to seek to benefit humanity, and to avoid the foolish factionalism to which we sometimes give ourselves.

The word translated as 'kindness' would, it may be useful to recall, have sounded in Greek something like 'Christ-ness'.

'Be outstanding in good works . . . avoid foolish speculations'. Do Christians today always manage this?

Final instructions

12-15 When I send Artemas or Tychicus to you, make an effort to come to me at Nicopolis; for it is there that I have decided to spend the winter. Send Zenas the lawyer and Apollos on their way with alacrity, so that nothing may be lacking to them. And let our people also learn to be outstanding in good works, to relieve essential needs, that they may not be unproductive.

All those who are with me greet you. Greet those who love us in faith. Grace be with you all.

The letter ends, as Pauline letters so often do, with various personal greetings and instructions; two of the four names here are unknown to us, nor do we know which Nicopolis this might be (it is the only time when the place is mentioned in the entire New Testament). Once again the Christians are exhorted to good works, apparently in favour of non-Christians.

The Letter to Philemon

The Letter to Philemon

This is a 'charming postcard' of a letter; there is no doubt about it having been written by Paul, though the reader will need to decide what is Onesimus's situation: Is he (as most people have assumed) a runaway slave? Or is he in some ways at odds with his master? Or did Philemon send Onesimus to look after Paul in prison, as some scholars have suggested recently? Or, as some argue, is the letter really addressed to Archippus? (See Colossians 4:9, 17 in support of this theory.)

Depending on your decision about that, you may want to consider the claim of some scholars that Paul here writes in a bullying, manipulative way, leaving Philemon no choice about his response.

Why do you think Paul does not here launch an attack on the institution of slavery?

Opening greetings (to a community, not an individual)

1-3 Paul, a prisoner of Christ Jesus, and Timothy our fellow Christian, to our beloved
Philemon, our co-worker, and to Apphia our sister and Archippus our fellow
campaigner, and to the church in your house, grace to you all and peace, from God
our Father and the Lord Jesus Christ.

Clearly we should be mistaken in supposing that this is just a private letter; it has two authors, and is addressed to Philemon, Apphia (Mrs Philemon?), Archippus, and an entire church; and the 'you' to whom the greetings are addressed is unmistakably plural, but the 'your' in the phrase 'the church in your house' is singular, and it follows the name of Archippus. Archippus is mentioned in Colossians 4:17 and Onesimus in Colossians 4:9. There are clear connections between the two letters.

Thanksgiving

4-7 I give thanks to my God, all the time making mention of you in my prayers, when
I hear of your love and your faith which you have in the Lord Jesus and towards all
the saints, so that the solidarity of your faith may become operative, in the knowledge
of all that is good in us, [turning us] to Christ. For I have had much joy and comfort
through your love; because the hearts of the saints have been refreshed through you,
my brother.

The thanksgiving is conventionally the second part of a letter in the ancient world, and, except in Galatians, Paul always followed the convention. That having been said, Paul is particularly grateful for some loving attention that Philemon (or Archippus) has shown, which is variously characterised as 'joy', 'comfort', and (a phrase that we shall meet again) 'refreshing the hearts of the saints'.

Paul's request – Part I (but what is he asking for?)

8-14 Therefore, although I have full authority to command you to do what is your duty, because of [my] love, I [would] rather ask you, being who I am, Paul, an old man, and now a prisoner of Christ Jesus. I am asking you about my child, whom I have fathered in prison, Onesimus, the one who was once Useless to you, but is now Useful to both you and me, whom I am sending you, that is my heart, whom I should have liked to keep for myself, so that in your place he might serve me in my gospel-prison; but without your consent I didn't want to do anything, so that your good deed should not be done under compulsion, but willingly.

The standard interpretation of the request in Philemon has been that Paul is asking the slave-owner to be nice to the returned runaway slave, and not punish him as he deserves. An alternative reading is to understand it as the rather more radical demand, that Onesimus be set free and returned to Paul.

It is clear that Paul wants something, and that he is applying some pressure to get it. He stresses that he is 'an old man and a prisoner', in a bid for sympathy. Another tactic is some witty wordplay. The slave's name is Onesimus, given emphasis by the position it has in the sentence. Now the name means 'profitable', and right next to it, Paul places two adjectives to refer to 'profitable', namely 'useless' and 'useful', whose significance we have tried to emphasise by the use of capitals. It does not stop there, however; for the sound of the two words in Greek would have suggested something like 'Christ-less', and 'Christ-well'. Paul is using a number of stratagems, including puns and a scarcely veiled reference to his authority. Another wordplay is involved in calling Onesimus 'my heart'; Paul has already said that Philemon (or Archippus) 'refreshes the hearts of the saints'; now Paul wants a piece of the action.

The request – Part II

15-20 For perhaps this was the reason that he was separated from you for a while, in order that you might have him back for all eternity, no longer as a slave, but as [something] more than a slave, a much-loved fellow Christian, beloved especially by me, and how much more by you, both in the flesh and in the Lord, So, if you regard me as a partner, accept him as though it were me. But ***if*** he has done you some wrong, owes you anything, put it down to my account. I, PAUL, AM WRITING IN MY OWN HAND, I SHALL REPAY. (I don't want to be telling you that you owe yourself to me!)

Yes, my brother, let me have this profit in the Lord. Refresh my heart in Christ.

What precisely does Paul want? It is impossible to be sure from what he writes whether he wants Onesimus's freedom so that he can return to be Paul's collaborator, or whether it is simply a matter of the slave-owner not exacting the draconian penalty to which he was entitled. One might in any case suppose that after this has been read out to the Church it would be extremely difficult for Philemon/Archippus not to give Onesimus his freedom.

The word that we have translated as 'partner' is from the koinonia *root, meaning union, communion, fellowship, solidarity, and so on. When Paul says 'if he has done you some wrong' he might mean not 'if (as you suggest)', but 'given that he has done you some wrong (as you and I are both well aware)'; so Onesimus has not necessarily robbed his boss.*

There are two more wordplays here: 'let me have this profit' is a play on Onesimus's name, and 'refresh my heart in Christ' is the third use in the letter of this idea of 'refreshing', which was first employed for what Philemon/ Archippus does for the saints. It is clearly part of Paul's tactics here.

Do you think that Philemon (or Archippus) would have refused to do what Paul wants? Could he have done so?

Concluding remarks

21-25 I am writing to you, confident in your obedience, knowing that you will do even more than what I say. But at the same time, prepare a guest room for me; for I am hoping that through your prayers I shall be given to you as a free gift.

Epaphras my fellow prisoner sends greetings in Christ Jesus, [as do] Mark, Aristarchus, Demas and Luke, my fellow workers.

The grace of the Lord Jesus Christ be with the spirit of you all.

Paul ends the letter with some hidden menace, perhaps. He is asking for obedience (and then some), but he has not precisely formulated a command. He is also hinting that he may be with them soon ('prepare a guest room for me'), so despite the imprisonment they may need to get something done.

'Given . . . as a free gift'. This is how God always gives and what is expected of the slave-owners.

Some readers think that Paul is not 'playing fair' here. Do you agree?

Maps

Palestine of the New Testament
Herod's Fortress
THE GREAT SEA
SYRO-PHOENICIA
GALILEE
Tyre
Ptolemais (Akko)
Mt Carmel
Caesarea Philippi (Paneas)
Trachonitis
Lake Huleh
Batanea
Gaulanitis
Cadas
Gischala
Chorazin
Capernaum
Gennesaret
Bethsaida-Julias
Dion
Magdala
Sea of Galilee
Gergesa
Asochis
Cana
Tiberias
Sepphoris
Abila
Nazareth
R. Yarmuk
Mt Tabor
Dora
Plain of Esdraelon
Nain
Crocodilon
Caesarea Maritima
DECAPOLIS
Pella
SAMARIA
Aenon
R. Jordan
Plain of Sharon
Sebaste (Samaria)
Gerasa
Mt Ebal
Sychar
Mt Gerizim
R. Jabbok
PERAEA
Antipatris
Jaffa
Gadara
Arimathaea
Philadelphia
Lydda
Ephraim
Jamnia
Jericho
Emmaus
Betharamphtha
Jerusalem
Ein-Kerem
Bethpage
Bethany
Qumran
Azotus
JUDAEA
Bethlehem
Ashkelon
Marisa
Bethsura
Gaza
Hebron
Dead Sea
En-gedi
R. Arnon
NABATAEAN KINGDOM
IDUMAEA
Masada

SICILY
MALTA
MACEDONIA
THRACE
Thessalonica
Amphipolis
Philippi
Neapolis
Apolloaia
Beroea
Larisa
Athens
Corinth
Cenchreae
ACHAIA
Troas
Assos
ASIA
Smyrna
Ephesus
Miletus
BITHYNIA & PONTUS
PHRYGIA
GALATIA
CAPPADOCIA
Antioch
Iconium
Lystra
LYCAONIA
PISIDIA
Derbe
Tarsus
PAMPHYLIA
Perga
Attalia
Patara
CILICIA
Seleucia
Antioch
SYRIA
RHODES
CYPRUS
Salamis
Paphos
THE GREAT SEA
CRETE
Tyre
Ptolemais
Caesarea
Jerusalem
NABATAEA
EGYPT
Paul's first journey
Paul's second journey
Paul's third journey

NOTES

NOTES